A-Z CHICHESTER

Key to Map Pages	2-3	Inde
		Villa
Map Pages	4-45	sele

REFEREN

A Road	A259	Car Park (selected)	🅿
B Road	B2178	Church or Chapel	†
Dual Carriageway		Cycleway (selected)	• • • 🚲 • •
One-way Street	➤	Fire Station	■
Traffic flow on A roads is also indicated by a heavy line on the driver's left.	➤	Hospital	Ⓗ
Road Under Construction		House Numbers (A & B Roads only)	10 124
Opening dates are correct at the time of publication.		Information Centre	🄸
Proposed Road		National Grid Reference	504
Restricted Access		Police Station	▲
Pedestrianized Road		Post Office	★
Track		Safety Camera with Speed Limit	㉚
Footpath		Fixed cameras and long term road works cameras. Symbols do not indicate camera direction.	
Residential Walkway		Toilet:	
Railway	Level Crossing Station	without facilities for the Disabled	▽
		with facilities for the Disabled	▽
Built-up Area	EAST LA	Educational Establishment	⬛
		Hospital or Healthcare Building	⬛
Local Authority Boundary	— • — • —	Industrial Building	⬛
National Park Boundary		Leisure or Recreational Facility	⬛
Posttown Boundary		Place of Interest	⬛
Postcode Boundary (within posttown)	— — —	Public Building	⬛
		Shopping Centre or Market	⬛
Map Continuation	18	Other Selected Buildings	⬛

SCALE

1:15,840
4 inches (10.16 cm) to 1 mile
6.31cm to 1 km

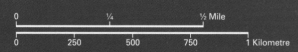

0 ¼ ½ Mile

0 250 500 750 1 Kilometre

EDITION 5 2014

Copyright © Geographers' A-Z Map Co. Ltd.

Telephone: 01732 781000 (Enquiries & Trade Sales)
01732 783422 (Retail Sales)

© Crown copyright and database rights 2013 Ordnance Survey 100017302.

Safety camera information supplied by www.PocketGPSWorld.com.
Speed Camera Location Database Copyright 2013 © PocketGPSWorld.com

A-Z A̶Z̶ AtoZ

registered trade marks of
Geographers' A-Z Map Company Ltd

www./az.co.uk

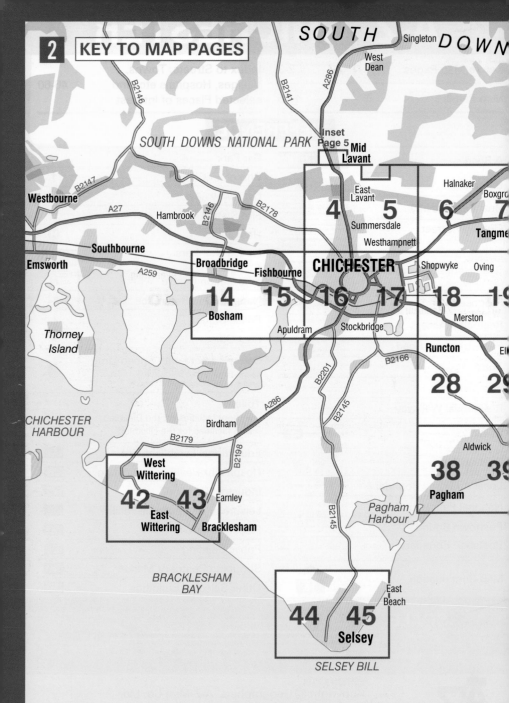

2 **KEY TO MAP PAGES**

SOUTH DOWN
Singleton
West Dean

SOUTH DOWNS NATIONAL PARK

Inset Page 5

Mid Lavant

Halnaker
Boxgro

Westbourne
B2147
Hambrook
B2146
B2178
East Lavant

4
5
6
7

Summersdale
Westhampnett
Tangme

A27

Southbourne

Emsworth
A259

Broadbridge
Fishbourne
CHICHESTER
Shopwyke
Oving

14
15
16
17
18
19

Bosham
Apuldram
Stockbridge
Merston

Thorney Island
B2201
B2166
Runcton
El

28
29

CHICHESTER HARBOUR
Birdham
B2179
A286
B2145

Aldwick

West Wittering
B2198
38
39

42
43
Earnley
B2145
Pagham

East Wittering
Bracklesham
Pagham Harbour

BRACKLESHAM BAY

East Beach

44
45
Selsey

SELSEY BILL

ENGLISH

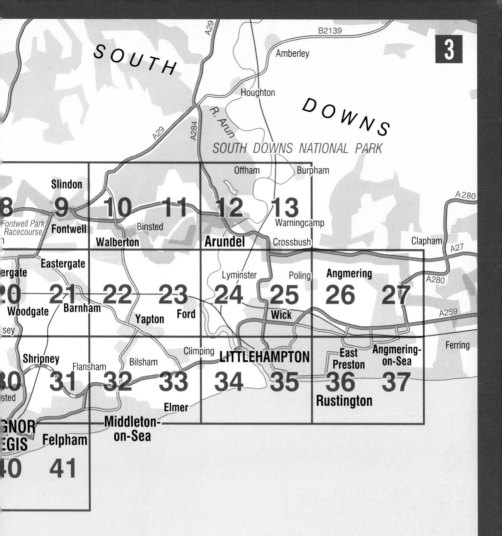

3

SOUTH

DOWNS

Amberley

Houghton

R. Arun

SOUTH DOWNS NATIONAL PARK

Offham Burpham

Slindon

Fontwell Park
Racecourse

8 **9** **10** **11** **12** **13**

Fontwell Binsted Warningcamp

Walberton **Arundel**

Crossbush Clapham

Eastergate

ergate **20** **21** **22** **23** **24** **25** **26** **27**

Woodgate Barnham Lyminster Poling **Angmering**

Yapton Ford **Wick**

sey

Ferring

Shripney Climbing **LITTLEHAMPTON** East Angmering-
Preston on-Sea

Flansham Bilsham

30 **31** **32** **33** **34** **35** **36** **37**

sted Elmer **Rustington**

GNOR
EGIS Felpham Middleton-
on-Sea

40 **41**

CHANNEL

SCALE		
0	1	2 Miles
0	1 2	3 Kilometres

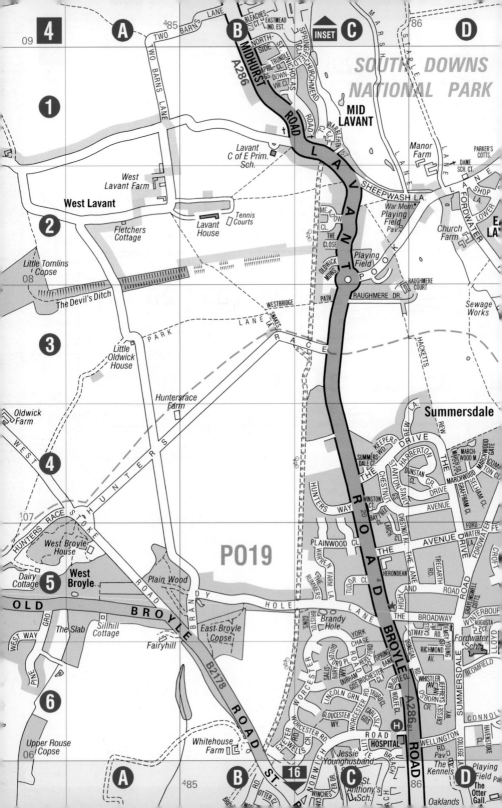

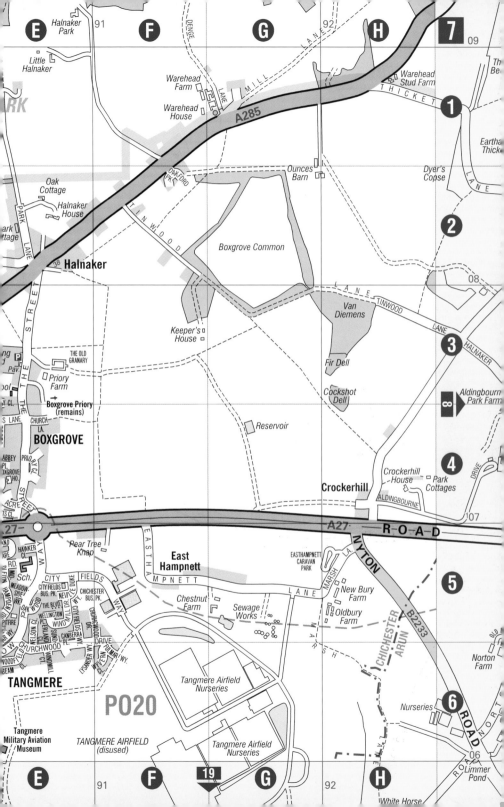

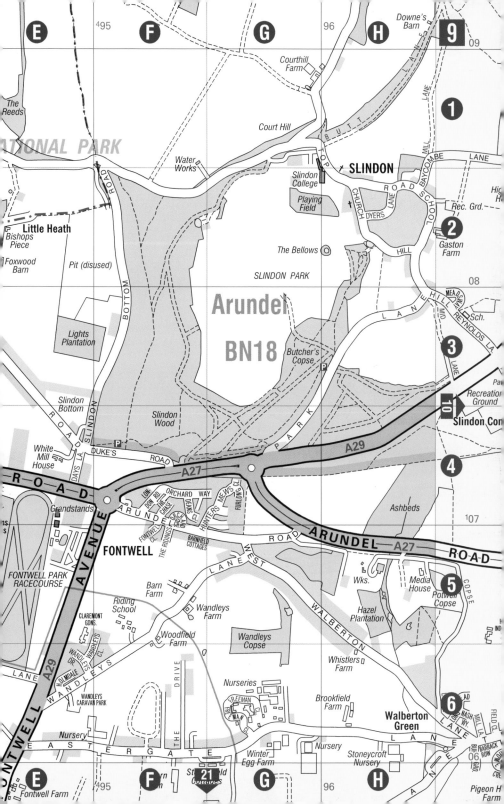

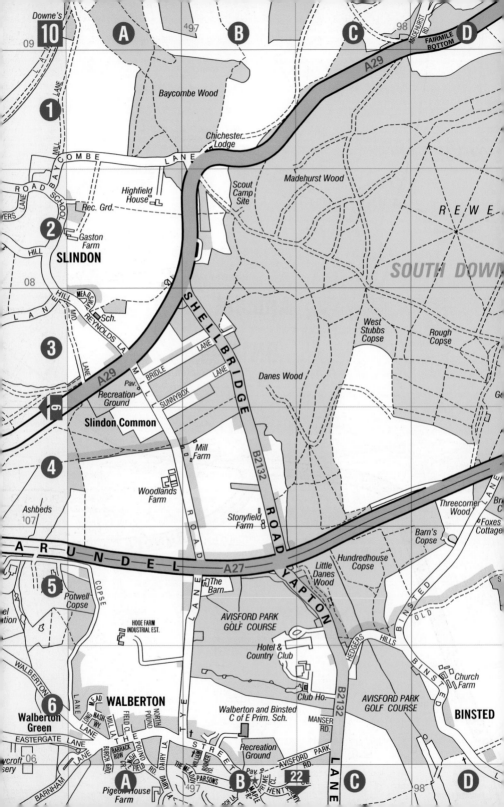

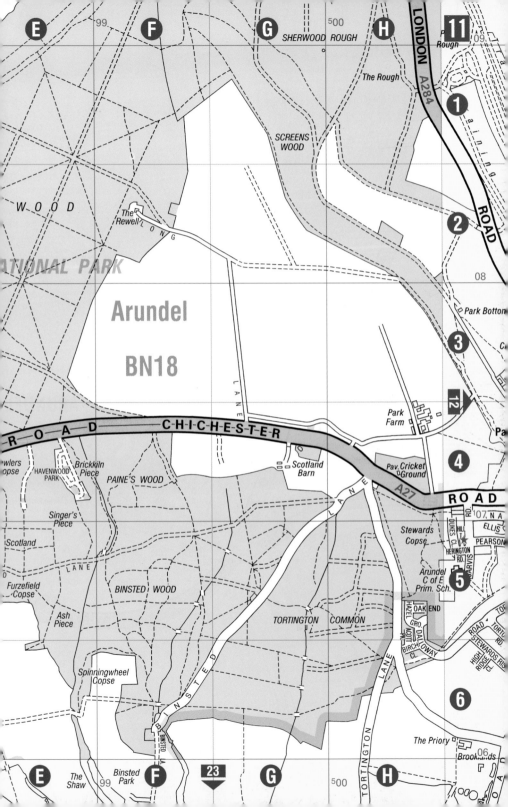

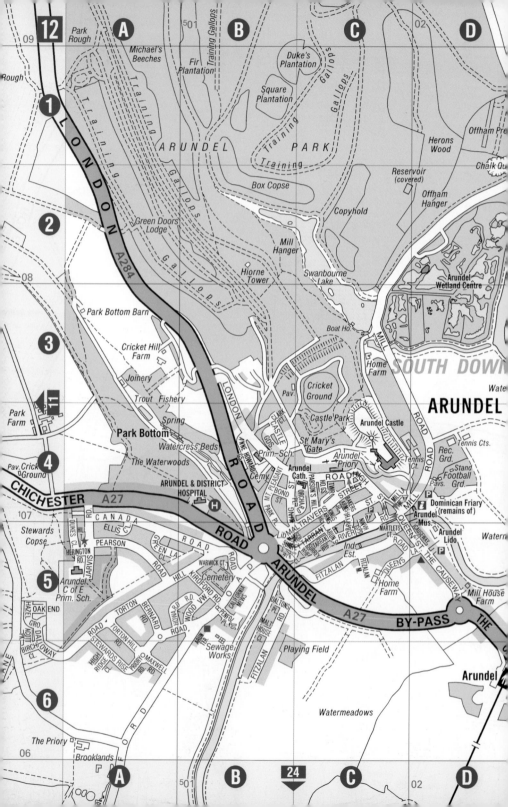

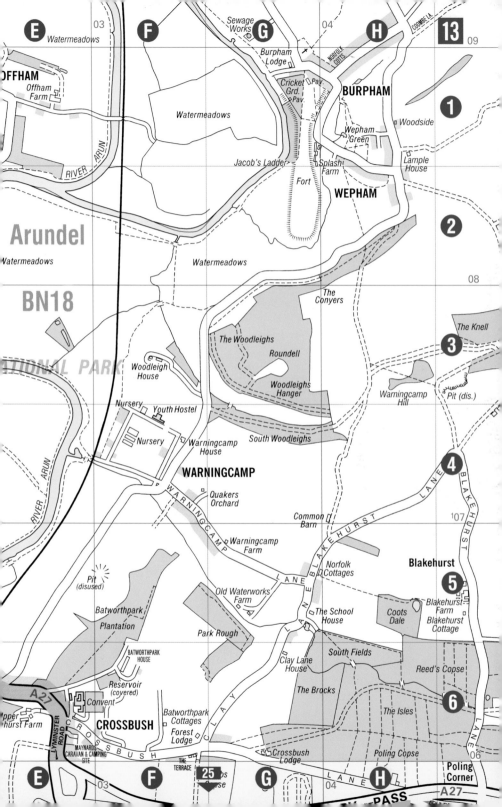

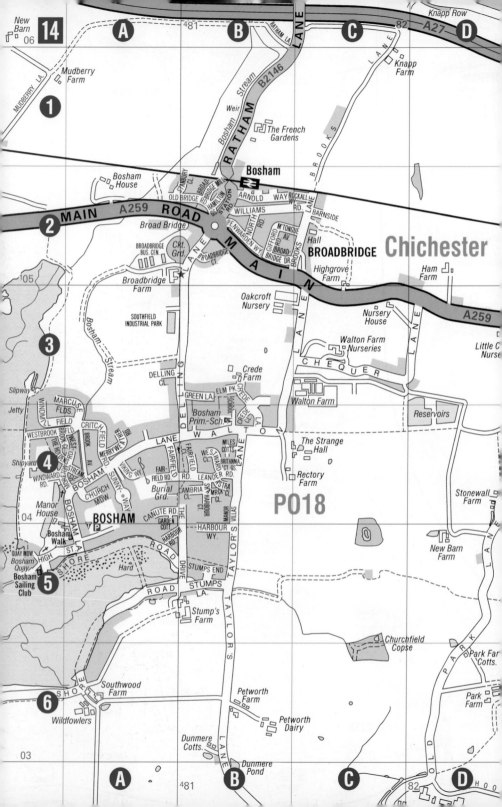

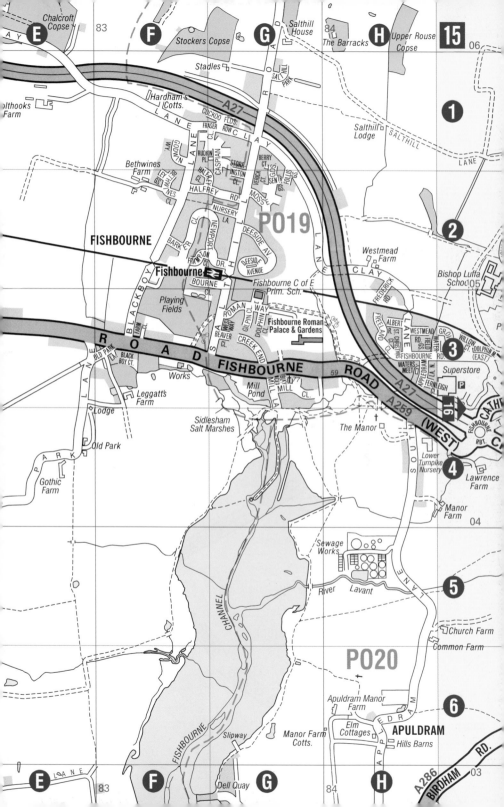

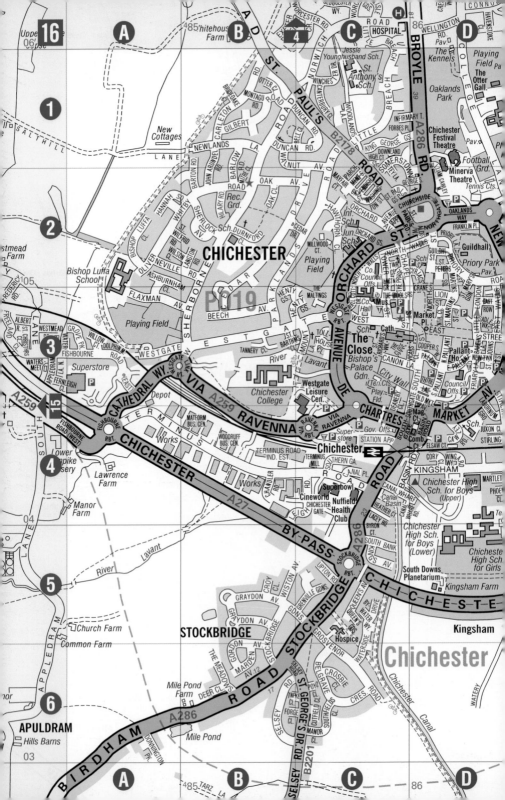

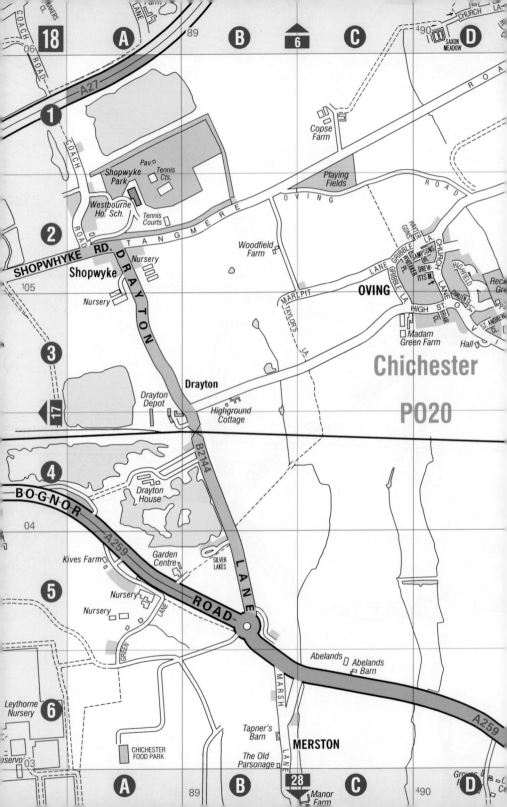

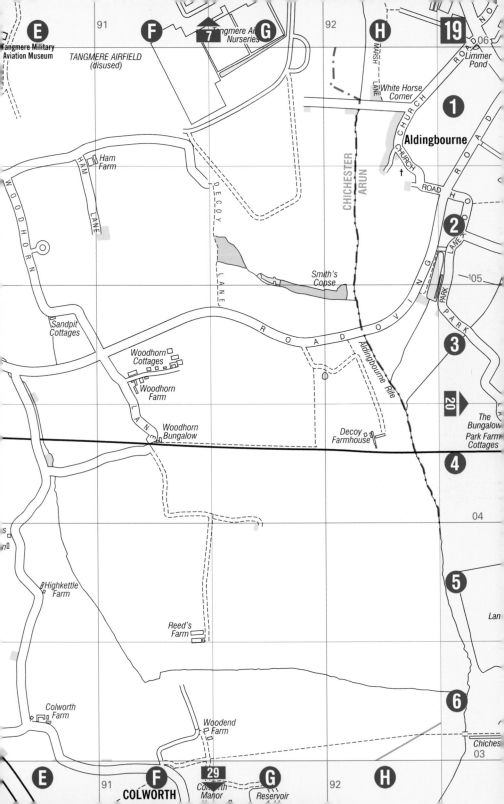

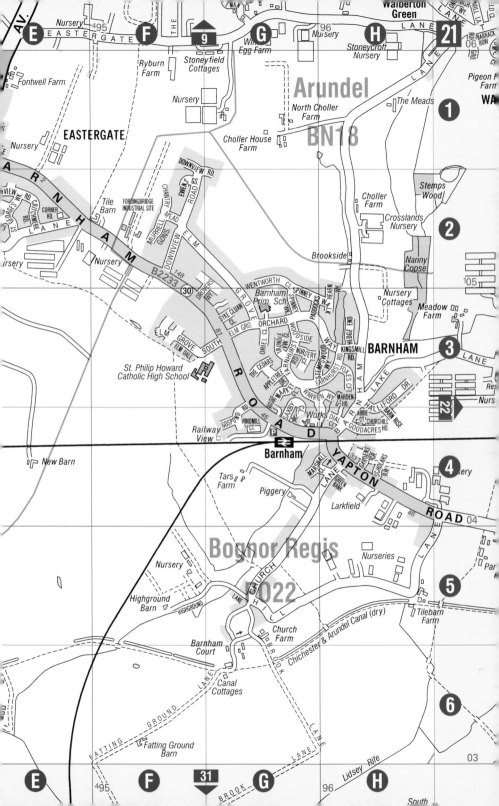

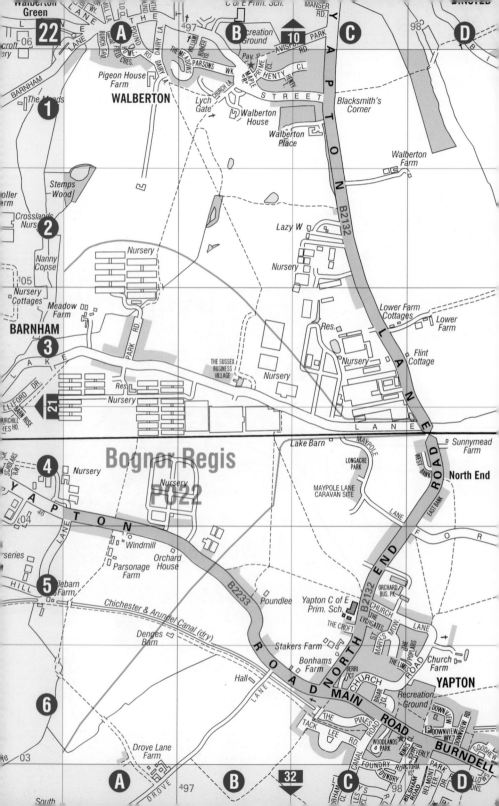

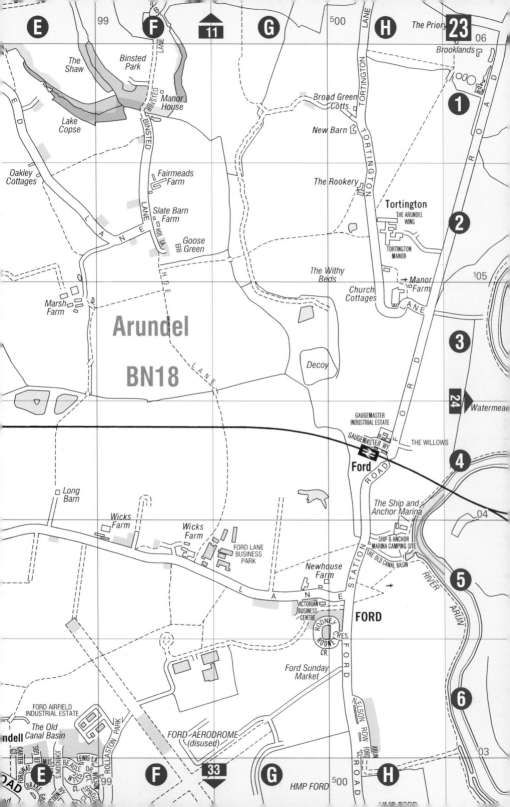

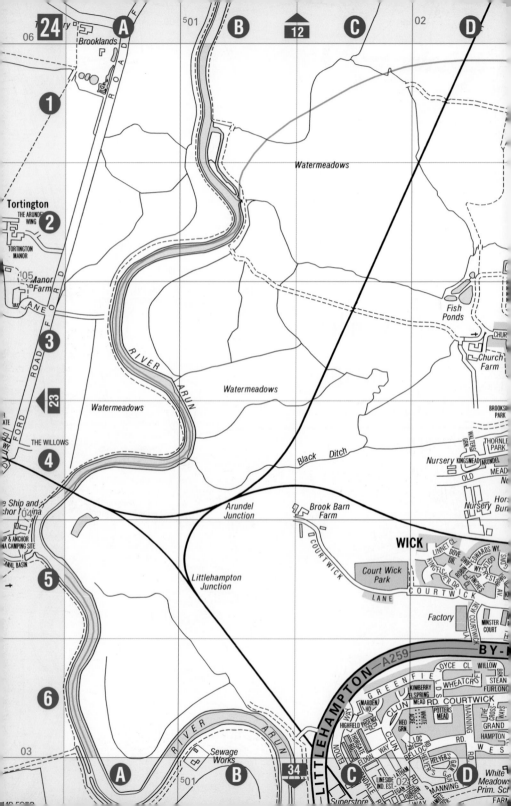

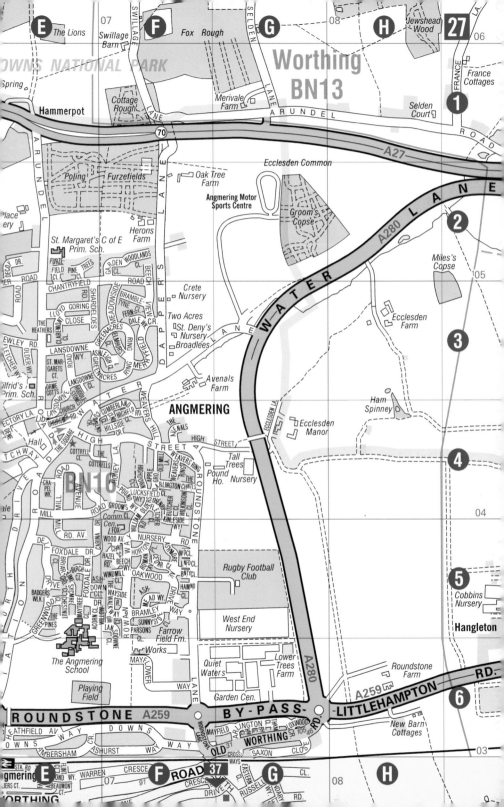

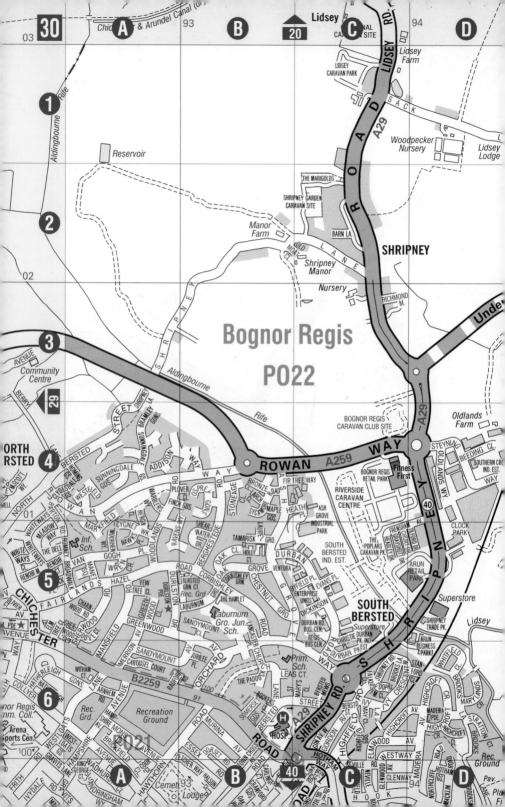

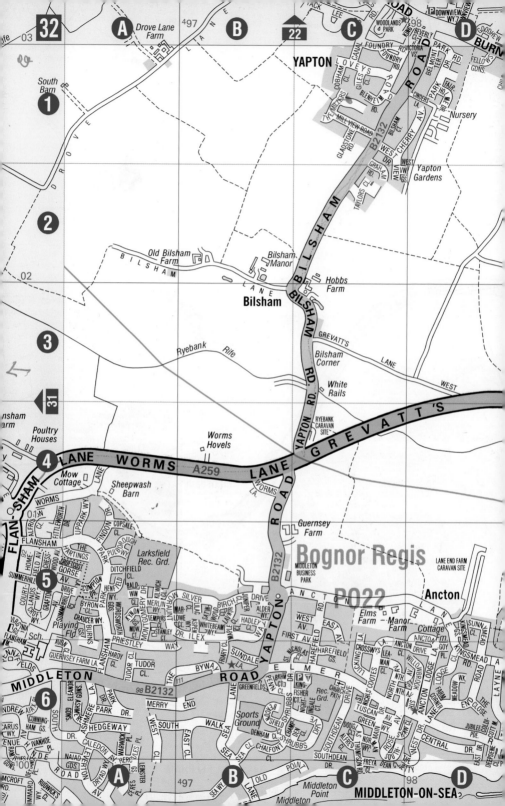

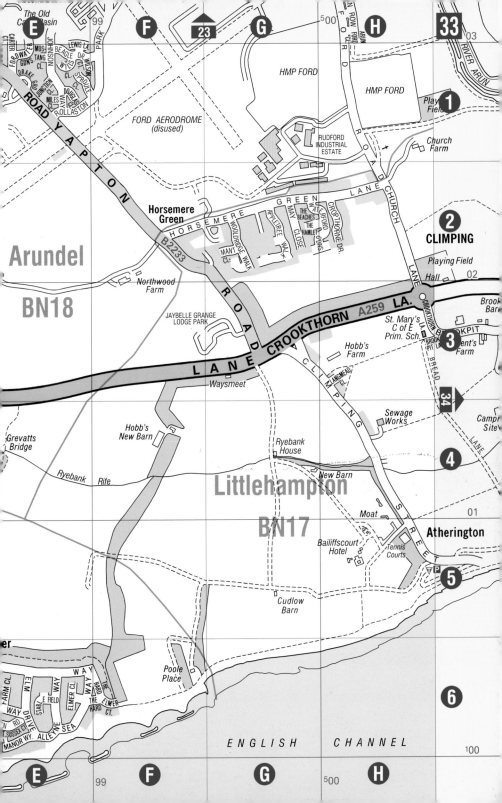

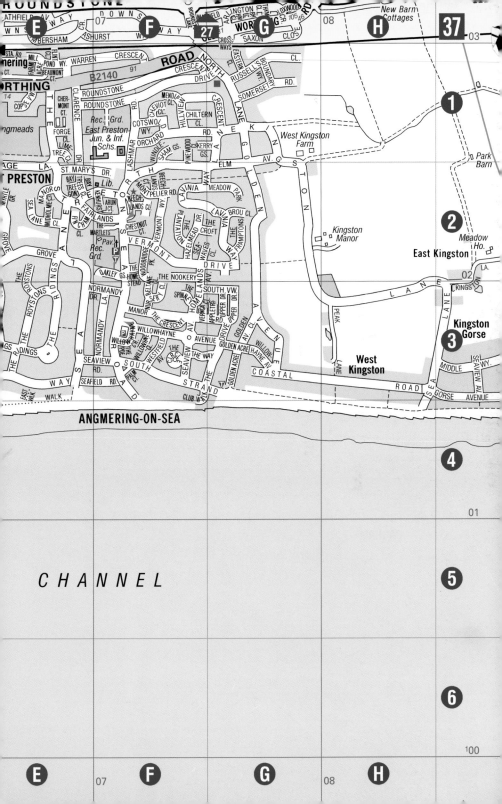

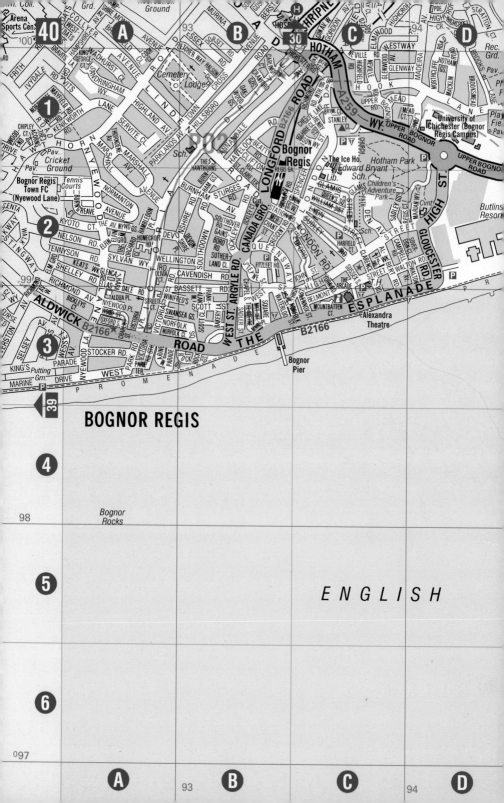

BOGNOR REGIS

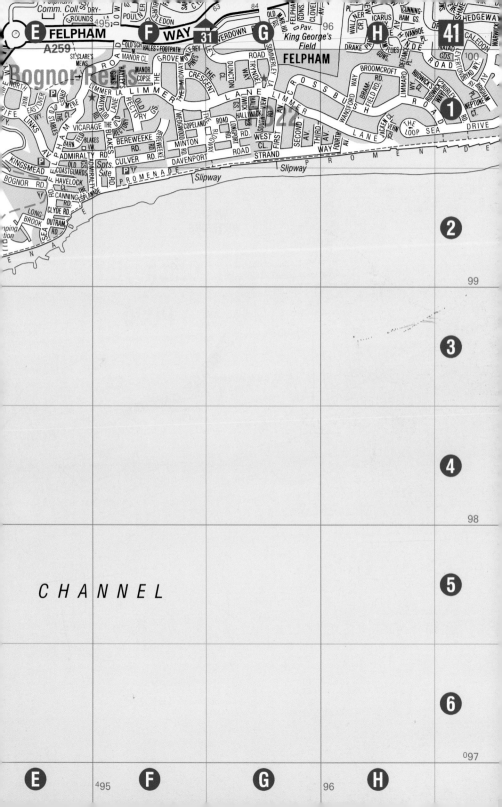

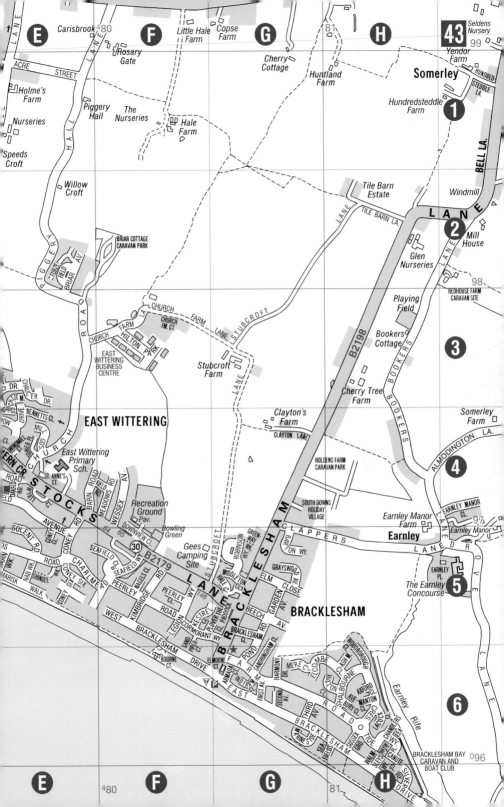

Carisbrook 480

Little Hale Farm

Copse Farm

Cherry Cottage

81

Seldens Nursery

Yendor Farm

Rosary Gate

Huntland Farm

Somerley

Hundredsteddle Farm

HUNDRED-STEDDLE LA.

1

ACRE STREET

Holme's Farm

Piggery Hall

The Nurseries

Hale Farm

BELL LA.

Nurseries

Speeds Croft

Willow Croft

HALL LANE

Tile Barn Estate

TILE BARN LA.

LANE

Windmill

2

Mill House

PIGGERY

BRIAR AV.

Briar Cottage Caravan Park

TURTLE FIELD

Glen Nurseries

LANE

B2198

Redhouse Farm Caravan Site

98

ROAD

CHURCH

CHURCH FARM LA.

CHURCH FM. CT.

FARM LANE

STUBCROFT

Playing Field

Bookers Cottage

CHURCH

FARM LA.

HILTON PARK

EAST WITTERING BUSINESS CENTRE

Stubcroft Farm

LANE

BOOKERS

3

DR.

CHASE M.

CHALFONT DR.

EAST WITTERING

Clayton's Farm

CLAYTON LANE

Cherry Tree Farm

Somerley Farm

ALMODINGTON LA.

4

CHASE M.

MILL

East Wittering Primary Sch.

HOLDENS FARM CARAVAN PARK

EARNLEY MANOR CL.

Earnley Manor

97

STOCKS

CHURCH

ST. ANNE'S CT.

BARN ROAD

MEADOWS RD.

WESSEX AV.

Recreation Ground Pav.

DOWNVIEW CL.

Bowling Green

GREEN-WAY WK.

ROBINSON

CL.

CLAPPERS

BARTON WY.

South Downs Holiday Village

Earnley Manor Farm

Earnley

LANE

EARNLEY DR.

GROVE

AVENUE

SOLENT RD.

CONEY RD.

CHARLMEAD

SEAFIELD CL.

CONEY SIX

B2179

ST. LUCROFT

MIDDLETON

GREEN-WAY

ELM CL.

GARDEN AV.

GRAYSWOOD AV.

CLOSE

EARNLEY PL.

The Earnley Concourse

5

MARISK

SHINGLE

WK.

NAB WK.

CONEY

ROAD

PEERLEY RD.

MAGELS CL.

KIMBRIDGE CL.

SEAFIELD CL.

30

LANE

PEERLEY CL.

VESTRY

PLOVERS CL.

THE PADDOCK

BEECH AV.

BRACKLESHAM

WEST

BRACKLESHAM

LEGION WY.

CORMORANT WY.

PREPARATORY

SANDPIPER CL.

BRACKLESHAM CL.

POND

WINDBROUGH CL.

CLASH CL.

HARMONY

Gees Camping Site

BOURNE CT.

DRIVE

FARM

ELMDENE CT.

ARMADA

OLD LN.

EAST

ROAD

FIRST AV.

SECOND AV.

MERE CL.

ELCOMBE

SHALBOURNE AV.

BURY CL.

MANTON

AXFORD

Earnley Rife

6

P

THIRD AV.

BRACKLESHAM

PINES CL.

SEA

REEDS

SUSSEX CL.

TIDE

TIDEWAY

WALM CL.

CANUTE WY.

LADOCK

CHANDLERS

SILVER DRIVE

BRACKLESHAM BAY CARAVAN AND BOAT CLUB

096

E · 86 · F · G · 87 · H · **45** ·095

Coles Farm
Norton Corner
Lydiate
Greenlease Farm
Grange Farm
Bird Reserve

The Spit

❶

RECTORY LANE · GRANGE LANE

B2145

Works

PARK

Four Ways

Park Farm Cotts. · Park Farm

Bird Reserve

COPSE

Inner Owers

❷

94

UPWAYS CL.
HUNNISETT CL.
COLER CL.
PETTS RD.
ROBINSON CL.
WILLINGTON DR.
ELLIS SQ.
SHERRINGTON MEWS
ELLIS SQ.
ELLIS

Sports Ground

MANOR FARM CL.
D. MSHARE RD.
ST. GEORGES CL.
BROOMFIELD CL.
THE WILLOWS
KINGS CL.
FARM CT.
TREE CL.

DRIFT LANE

WHEATFIELD RD.

East Beach

PARK ROAD
PARK LANE
NEWFIELD CR.

LANE · PARK

EAST BEACH ROAD

❸

ST CHICHESTER
THE WILLOWS
PETER'S
RUNDLE

MOUNTWOOD RD.
ALLANDALE CL.
THE ROOKERY
BEACH

ELM WY.
HARCOURT WY.
FONTWELL WY.
CHICHESTER WAY
GILL WAY
ROUND STONE
WILFRED'S CL.

THE CLOSE

❸

CHURCH ROAD
WELLINGTON GDS.
ROBINS CL.
DENNY'S CL.
GOODWOOD CT.
EASTPOINT

ORCHARD PDE
OXFORD
DRIVE
ORPEN PL.
ROMNEY CL.
MANFIELD

BEACH RD.
EAST RD.
CONSTABLE DR.
ORMEROD DR.

EAST
PARK
ROAD
VIEW

Slipway

❹

SEAL PRIM. ACADEMY
NETHER CL.
HOUSE CL.
EGLEN CRES.

NORTH ROAD
GAINSBOROUGH RD.
LAND CL.
SLATSFIELD CL.
NORTHFIELD CL.
LINGFIELD WAY
AGNES CL.
HANVER CL.

MERRYFIELD DR.
EAST BANK
FRASER CL.
RUSKIN CL.
BEVERLEY
DRIVE

MARINE DRIVE
BROAD

SWAY

93

OLD BAKERY M.
WESTERN RD.
CHAYLE GDS.
SUNNYMEAD DR.
FISHERMANS WK.
SUNNYMEAD
BRIXTON CL.

LAND RD.
ALBION

ROAD · MANOR STREET

❹

WINDSOR RD.
LAWRENCE CL.
BEACON DRIVE
JONES SQ.
JAMES STREET

The Lifeboat Mus.
Lifeboat Station

E N G L I S H

❺

THE BARN RD.
LANE
MIXON CL.
PARKWAY
LIFEBOAT WAY

C H A N N E L

YORK RD.
GRAFTON ROAD
DOMEHSE CL.
WIGHT WY.
SPARS CL.
CANADIAN CRES.
BARNES CL.
PENNYCROFT CL.
OVAL LANE
Play. Fld.

❻

SELSEY BILL

92

E · 86 · F · G · 87 · H

INDEX

Including Streets, Places & Areas, Hospitals etc., Industrial Estates,
Selected Flats & Walkways, Stations and Selected Places of Interest.

HOW TO USE THIS INDEX

1. Each street name is followed by its Postcode District, then by its Locality abbreviation(s) and then by its map reference;
   e.g. **Abbotsbury** PO21: Pag . . . . 5B **38** is in the PO21 Postcode District and the Pagham Locality and is to be found in square 5B on page **38**.
   The page number is shown in bold type.

2. A strict alphabetical order is followed in which Av., Rd., St., etc. (though abbreviated) are read in full and as part of the street name;
   e.g. **Black Boy Ct.** appears after **Blackbird Way** but before **Blackboy La.**

3. Streets and a selection of flats and walkways that cannot be shown on the mapping, appear in the index with the thoroughfare to which they are connected
   shown in brackets; e.g. **Abingdon Lodge** BN16: Rust . . . . 2C **36** (off Ruston Av.)

4. Addresses that are in more than one part are referred to as not continuous.

5. Places and areas are shown in the index in BLUE TYPE and the map reference is to the actual map square in which the town centre or area is located and not
   to the place name shown on the map; e.g. ANCTON 6D 32

6. An example of a selected place of interest is **Arundel Castle** 4C 12

7. An example of a station is **Angmering Station (Rail)** 1E 37

8. An example of a Hospital, Hospice or selected Healthcare facility is **ARUNDEL & DISTRICT HOSPITAL** 4B 12

GENERAL ABBREVIATIONS

App. : Approach	**Gdns.** : Gardens	**Pas.** : Passage
Av. : Avenue	**Gth.** : Garth	**Pl.** : Place
Bri. : Bridge	**Ga.** : Gate	**Pct.** : Precinct
Bus. : Business	**Grn.** : Green	**Ri.** : Rise
Cen. : Centre	**Gro.** : Grove	**Rd.** : Road
Cir. : Circus	**Ho.** : House	**Rdbt.** : Roundabout
Cl. : Close	**Ind.** : Industrial	**Sth.** : South
Cnr. : Corner	**Info.** : Information	**Sq.** : Square
Cott. : Cottage	**La.** : Lane	**St.** : Street
Cotts. : Cottages	**Lwr.** : Lower	**Ter.** : Terrace
Ct. : Court	**Mnr.** : Manor	**Trad.** : Trading
Cres. : Crescent	**Mans.** : Mansions	**Up.** : Upper
Cft. : Croft	**Mdw.** : Meadow	**Va.** : Vale
Dr. : Drive	**Mdws.** : Meadows	**Vw.** : View
E. : East	**M.** : Mews	**Vs.** : Villas
Ent. : Enterprise	**Mt.** : Mount	**Wlk.** : Walk
Est. : Estate	**Mus.** : Museum	**W.** : West
Fld. : Field	**Nth.** : North	**Yd.** : Yard
Flds. : Fields	**Pde.** : Parade	
Gdn. : Garden	**Pk.** : Park	

LOCALITY ABBREVIATIONS

Ald : **Aldingbourne**	E Pres : **East Preston**	Pat : **Patching**
Aldw : **Aldwick**	E Witt : **East Wittering**	Poling : **Poling**
Ang : **Angmering**	E'gate : **Eastergate**	Runc : **Runcton**
Apul : **Apuldram**	Felp : **Felpham**	Rust : **Rustington**
Arun : **Arundel**	Fer : **Ferring**	Sel : **Selsey**
Barn : **Barnham**	Fish : **Fishbourne**	Shrip : **Shripney**
Bers : **Bersted**	Flan : **Flansham**	Sidle : **Sidlesham**
Bils : **Bilsham**	Font : **Fontwell**	Slind : **Slindon**
Bins : **Binsted**	Ford : **Ford**	S Mun : **South Mundham**
Bir : **Birdham**	Good : **Goodwood**	Tang : **Tangmere**
Bog R : **Bognor Regis**	Hal : **Halnaker**	Tort : **Tortington**
Bosh : **Bosham**	Huns : **Hunston**	Walb : **Walberton**
Box : **Boxgrove**	King G : **Kingston Gorse**	W'camp : **Warningcamp**
Brac : **Bracklesham**	Lag : **Lagness**	W Ash : **West Ashling**
Burp : **Burpham**	L'ton : **Littlehampton**	W Bro : **West Broyle**
Chich : **Chichester**	Lym : **Lyminster**	W Witt : **West Wittering**
Climp : **Climping**	Made : **Madehurst**	Westg : **Westergate**
Cross : **Crossbush**	Midd S : **Middleton-on-Sea**	Westh : **Westhampnett**
Donn : **Donnington**	Mid L : **Mid Lavant**	Wick : **Wick**
Earn : **Earnley**	N Mun : **North Mundham**	W'gate : **Woodgate**
Eart : **Eartham**	Nort : **Norton**	Yap : **Yapton**
E Ash : **East Ashling**	Oving : **Oving**	
E Lav : **East Lavant**	Pag : **Pagham**	

A

Abbie Ct. PO22: Barn .4H 21	**Admiralty Ct.** PO22: Felp 1E **41**	**Aldwick Av.** PO21: Aldw .3G **39**
Abbotswood BN16: Rust 1C **36**	(off Admiralty Rd.)	**Aldwick Cl.** BN16: Rust .4A **36**
Abbotswood Wlk.	**Admiralty Gdns.** PO22: Felp 1E **41**	**Aldwick Felds** PO21: Aldw 2F **39**
BN16: Rust 3B **36**	**Admiralty Rd.** PO22: Felp 1E **41**	**Aldwick Gdns.** PO21: Aldw 2G **39**
Abbottsbury PO21: Pag 5B **38**	**Admiralty Row** PO20: E Witt 4E **43**	**Aldwick Hundred** PO21: Aldw 4F **39**
Abbotts Cl. PO18: Box 4E **7**	(off Cakeham Rd.)	**Aldwick Pl.** PO21: Aldw 3G **39**
A'Becket's Av. PO21: Aldw 4C **38**	**Aigburth Av.** PO21: Aldw 2E **39**	**Aldwick Rd.**
Abercorn Wlk. PO20: E'gate 2D **20**	**Ajax Pl.** PO22: Felp 6H **31**	PO21: Aldw, Bog R 3F **39**
Aberdare Cl. PO19: Chich 1E **17**	**Albert Rd.** BN16: Rust 1B **36**	**Aldwick St.** PO21: Aldw 3F **39**
Abingdon Lodge BN16: Rust 2C **36**	BN17: L'ton 2E **35**	**Alexander Cl.** PO21: Aldw 3F **39**
(off Ruston Av.)	PO19: Chich 3H **15**	**Alexandra Rd.** PO19: Chich 2E **17**
Acorn Cl. BN16: Ang .5E **27**	PO21: Bog R 2C **40**	**Alexandra Ter.** PO21: Bog R 2C **40**
PO20: Sel 3C **44**	**Albion Rd.** PO20: Sel .5F **45**	(off Clarence Rd.)
Acorn End PO21: Aldw 3E **39**	**Alborough Way** PO21: Aldw 3E **39**	**Alexandra Theatre**
Acorns, The PO21: Bog R 1H **39**	**Aldbourne Dr.** PO21: Aldw 3E **39**	Bognor Regis .3C **40**
Acre Cl. BN16: Rust .1A **36**	**Aldermans Wlk.** PO19: Chich 2D **16**	**Alfred Cl.** PO22: Midd S 6C **32**
Acre St. PO20: W Witt 1E **43**	**Alder Way** PO22: Midd S 5B **32**	**Alfriston Cl.** PO22: Felp 5H **31**
Addison Way PO22: Bers 4A **30**	**ALDINGBOURNE** 1H **19**	**Allandale Cl.** PO20: Sel 3F **45**
Adelaide Rd. PO19: Chich 2E **17**	**Aldingbourne Dr.** PO18: Box 4H **7**	**Allangate Dr.** BN16: Rust 1C **36**
Admirals Wlk. BN17: L'ton 1H **35**	**Aldingbourne Ho.** PO18: Nort 4A **8**	**Alleyne Way** PO22: Midd S 6E **33**
	Aldingbourne Pk. PO20: Ald 4C **20**	**Allin Way** PO22: Felp .5G **31**
	Alding Cres. PO21: Bers 4G **29**	**Almodington La.** PO20: Earn 4H **43**
	ALDWICK 3F **39**	**Alperton Cl.** PO21: Aldw 3D **38**

Alpha Ct. *BN17: L'ton* *2D 34*
    (off Terminus Rd.)
Amberley Cl. BN17: Wick 1F 35
Amberley Dr. PO21: Bog R 1G 39
Amberley Rd. BN16: Rust 3B 36
Ambersham Cres. BN16: Ang 6E 27
Ambleside Cl. PO22: Felp 5G 31
Amelia Ct. PO20: E Witt 4D 42
Amenic Ct. *BN17: L'ton* *2F 35*
    (off Church St.)
Amstel Ct. *BN17: L'ton* *3G 35*
    (off Selborne Rd.)
Anchor Springs BN17: L'ton 2E 35
ANCTON 6D 32
Ancton Cl. PO22: Midd S 6C 32
Ancton Dr. PO22: Midd S 5D 32
Ancton La. PO22: Midd S 5C 32
Ancton Lodge La. PO22: Midd S 6D 32
Ancton Way PO22: Midd S 6D 32
Andrew Av. PO22: Felp 6H 31
Andrew Cl. BN16: Rust 1A 36
Angell Est. PO19: Chich 4F 17
ANGMERING 4E 27
Angmering La. BN16: E Pres 3D 36
Angmering Motor Sports Cen. 2G 27
ANGMERING-ON-SEA 3F 37
Angmering Station (Rail) 1E 37
Angmering Way BN16: Rust 6D 26
Annandale Av. PO21: Bog R 1B 40
Anne Howard Gdns. BN18: Arun 4B 12
Anson Rd. PO21: Aldw 3C 38
Answorth Cl. PO19: Chich 6E 5
Appledram La. Nth. PO19: Chich 3H 15
Appledram La. Sth. PO20: Apul, Fish 6H 15
Apple Gro. BN16: Ang 4F 27
    PO21: Aldw 4C 38
Appletree Dr. PO22: Barn 3G 21
Appletrees BN16: E Pres 3G 37
Appletree Wlk. BN17: Climp 2G 33
April Gdns. PO18: Mid L 1B 4
APULDRAM 6H 15
Arcade, The *BN17: L'ton* *2E 35*
    (off Arcade Rd.)
    PO21: Bog R 2C 40
Arcade Rd. BN17: L'ton 2E 35
Arena Sports Cen.
    Bognor Regis 6H 29
Argyle Cir. *PO21: Bog R* *2B 40*
    (off Argyle Rd.)
Argyle Rd. PO21: Bog R 3B 40
Arlington Cres. BN16: E Pres 6G 27
Armadale Rd. PO19: Chich 2E 17
Arndale Rd. BN17: Wick 1C 34
Arnell Av. PO20: Sel 4E 45
Arnhem Rd. PO21: Bog R 6A 30
Arnold Way PO18: Bosh 2B 14
Arran Ga. *PO21: Bog R* *2C 40*
    (off Marian Way)
Artex Av. BN16: Rust 6B 26
Arun Bus. Pk. PO22: Bers 5D 30
Arun Cl. BN16: Rust 1B 36
Arun Ct. BN16: E Pres 2F 37
ARUNDEL 4C 12
ARUNDEL & DISTRICT HOSPITAL 4B 12
Arundel Arts, Craft & Antique Market 4C 12
    (off Tarrant St.)
Arundel By-Pass BN18: Arun 5B 12
Arundel Castle 4C 12
Arundel Cathedral 4C 12
Arundel Cl. PO21: Bog R 1H 39
Arundel Dr. BN17: Wick 4D 24
Arundel Gdn. BN16: Rust 2B 36
Arundel Lido 5D 12
Arundel Mus. 4D 12
Arundel Rd. BN13: Pat 1E 27
    BN16: Ang 1E 27
    BN17: L'ton .1E 35
    BN18: Bins, Font, Slind, Walb 4F 9
    BN18: Poling 1A 26
    PO18: Box, Tang, Nort 5C 6
    PO20: Box, Tang 5C 6
Arundel Station (Rail) 6D 12
Arundel Way PO22: Midd S 6E 33
Arundel Wetland Cen. 2D 12
Arundel Wing, The BN18: Tort 2H 23
Arun Ford Cl. BN18: Ford 6H 23
Arun Leisure Cen. 6E 31
Arun Pde. BN17: L'ton 3E 35
Arun Retail Pk. PO22: Bers 5D 30
Arun Rd. PO21: Bog R 1H 39
Arun St. BN18: Arun 5C 12
Arun Ter. BN18: Arun 5B 12
Arun Way PO21: Aldw 5C 38
    (not continuous)
Arun Wharf *BN17: L'ton* *2D 34*
    (off River Rd.)
Arun Yacht Club .3E 35
Ascot Cl. PO20: W Witt 3E 43
Ascot Way BN16: Rust 1D 36
Ashbee Ct. PO21: Bers 4G 29
Ashbee Gdns. PO21: Bers 4G 29

Ashburnham Cl. PO19: Chich 2A 16
Ash Cl. BN17: L'ton 6H 25
Ashcroft Way PO21: Pag 5B 38
Ashdown Cl. BN16: Ang 5E 27
Ash Gro. PO22: Bers, Bog R 4B 30
Ash Gro. Ind. Pk. PO22: Bers 4C 30
Ash La. BN16: Rust 2B 36
Ashleigh Cl. BN16: Ang 3E 27
Ashmead Way BN16: Ang 5F 27
Ashmere Gdns. PO22: Felp 6A 32
Ashmere La. PO22: Felp 6A 32
Ashmore Av. BN16: Ang 5F 27
Ashmount Ho. *PO21: Bog R* *2B 40*
    (off Argyle Rd.)
Ashton Gdns. BN16: Rust 3B 36
Ashurst Cl. PO21: Bers 5H 29
Ashurst Way BN16: Ang 6E 27
Ashwood Dr. BN16: Rust 2B 36
Aspen Cl. BN17: L'ton 6H 25
Aspen Way PO22: Midd S 5B 32
Astra Cl. PO18: Bosh 4B 14
ATHERINGTON 5H 33
Atlantic Ho. *BN16: Rust* *3A 36*
    (off Harsfold Cl.)
Augusta Ct. PO19: Chich 5D 4
Avebury Cl. PO20: Brac 6H 43
Avenals, The BN16: Ang 4F 27
Avenue, The PO19: Chich 5C 4
Avenue App. PO19: Chich 2C 16
Avenue de Chartres PO19: Chich 3C 16
Avenue de Chartres Rdbt. *PO19: Chich* . . .*3C 16*
    (off Avenue de Chartres)
Avian Gdns. PO21: Pag 3G 38
Avisford Pk. Golf Course 6C 10
Avisford Pk. Rd. BN18: Walb 6B 10
Avisford Ter. *PO21: Aldw* *2E 39*
    (off Rose Grn. Rd.)
Avon Cl. PO22: Felp 6H 31
Avon Rd. BN17: L'ton 2E 35
Axford Cl. PO20: Brac 6H 43

B

Babsham La. PO21: Bers 3G 29
Badgers Wlk. BN16: Ang 5E 27
Badger Wlk. *PO19: Chich* *1F 17*
    (off Swanfield Dr.)
Baffins Ct. *PO19: Chich* *3D 16*
    (off Baffins La.)
Baffins La. PO19: Chich 3D 16
Bailey Cl. *BN17: L'ton* *6H 25*
    (off Lanyards)
Bakers Arms Hill BN18: Arun 4C 12
Bakery La. PO21: Bog R 3B 40
Bala Cres. PO22: Felp 5G 31
Baldwin Cl. PO22: Midd S 5A 32
Balliol Cl. PO22: Midd S 1F 39
Balmoral Cl. BN16: Rust 6A 26
    PO19: Chich 3G 17
    PO21: Aldw .3F 39
Banjo Rd. BN17: L'ton 4F 35
Bankview Cl. PO22: Bog R 1C 40
Barford Rd. PO19: Chich 4D 16
Barker Cl. PO18: Fish 2F 15
Barley Cl. PO21: Pag 3B 38
Barlow Rd. PO19: Chich 2B 16
Barn Cl. BN17: Wick 5F 25
Barncroft Cl. PO20: Tang 6D 6
Barnes Cl. PO20: Sel 6E 45
Barnett Cl. PO20: E'gate 1D 20
Barnett's Fld. PO20: Westg 2C 20
Barn Feld PO22: Felp 1E 41
Barnfield Cotts. BN18: Nort 5F 9
Barnfield Dr. PO19: Chich 1E 17
BARNHAM 4G 21
Barnham La. BN18: Walb 4H 21
    PO22: Barn .4H 21
Barnham Rd. PO20: Barn, E'gate 1E 21
    PO22: Barn, E'gate 1E 21
Barnham Station (Rail) 4G 21
Barn La. PO22: Shrip 2C 30
Barn Ri. PO22: Barn 4H 21
Barn Rd. PO20: E Witt 4E 43
Barnside PO18: Bosh 2C 14
Barnsite Cl. BN16: Rust 1A 36
Barnsite Gdns. BN16: Rust 1A 36
Barn Wlk. PO20: E Witt 5E 43
Barons Cl. PO20: Westg 2C 20
Barons Mead PO21: Pag 5B 38
Barque Cl. BN17: L'ton 1H 35
Barrack La. PO21: Aldw 4E 39
Barrack Row BN18: Walb 6A 10
Barton Cl. PO21: Pag 4B 38
Barton Ct. BN16: Rust 2A 36
Barton Rd. PO19: Chich 2B 16
    PO22: Bers .2B 16
Barton Way PO20: Brac 5G 43
Barwick Cl. BN16: Rust 6A 26
Basin Rd. PO19: Chich 4C 16
Bassett Rd. PO21: Bers 3B 40
Bastion Ho. PO19: Chich 3D 16

Batworthpark Ho. BN18: Cross 6F 13
Baxendale Rd. PO19: Chich 1E 17
Bay Bri. Cres. PO22: Felp 4G 31
Baycombe La. BN18: Slind 2H 9
Bayford Rd. BN17: L'ton 3E 35
Bayley Rd. PO20: Tang 6D 6
Bayton Ct. PO19: Chich 3E 17
Baytree Cl. PO19: Chich 4C 4
Bay Tree Gdn. BN16: E Pres 2E 37
Bay Trees Cl. BN16: E Pres 2E 37
Bay Wlk. PO21: Aldw 5D 38
Beach Cl. PO21: Aldw 4D 38
Beach Ct. *BN17: L'ton* *3F 35*
    (off Irvine Rd.)
Beach Cres. BN17: L'ton 4F 35
Beaches, The BN17: Climp 2G 33
Beach Gdns. PO20: Sel 6D 44
    (not continuous)
Beach Rd. BN17: L'ton 2E 35
    PO20: Sel 3F 45
    (not continuous)
    PO21: Pag 6B 38
Beacon Dr. PO20: Sel 5E 45
Beaconsfield Cl. PO22: Midd S 6B 32
Beaconsfield Rd. BN17: Wick 6E 25
Beacon Way BN17: L'ton 1H 35
Beagle Dr. BN18: Ford 1E 33
Beatty Rd. PO21: Bog R 1B 40
Beaufield Cl. PO20: Sel 5D 44
Beaumont Ct. BN16: E Pres 1E 37
Beaumont Pk. BN17: L'ton 3H 35
Beaver Cl. PO19: Fish 3G 15
Bedencroft PO21: Aldw 2H 39
Bedford Av. PO21: Bers 5H 29
Bedford St. PO21: Bog R 2C 40
Beech Av. PO19: Chich 3B 16
    PO20: Brac .5G 43
Beech Cl. PO20: Westg 2C 20
    PO21: Pag 2A 38
Beechfield Pk. PO20: Ald 4B 20
Beechlands Cl. BN16: E Pres 2F 37
Beechlands Ct. BN16: E Pres 2F 37
Beech Vw. BN16: Ang 2F 27
Beeding Cl. PO22: Bers 4D 30
Belgrave Cres. PO19: Chich 6C 16
Bell Cl. PO19: Chich 1C 16
Bell Ct. PO21: Aldw 3D 38
Bell Davies Rd. BN17: L'ton 1G 35
Belle Meade Cl. PO20: Westg 4C 20
Bell La. PO20: Earn, Bir, E Witt 1H 43
Belloc Rd. BN17: Wick 6D 24
Bellscroft Cl. PO21: Bers 1G 35
Belmont St. PO21: Bog R 3C 40
Belmont Ter. BN18: Yap 1D 32
Beltane Cl. BN16: E Pres 3F 37
Belyngham Cres. BN17: Wick 1D 34
Benizi Ct. *PO21: Bog R* *2C 40*
    (off Clarence Rd.)
Bennetts Cl. PO20: W Witt 4E 43
Bentley Cl. BN16: Ang 5F 27
Ben Turner Ind. Est. PO19: Chich 3G 17
Bereweeke Rd. PO22: Felp 1F 41
Berghestede Rd. PO22: Bers 5B 30
Berkeley Ct. *PO21: Bog R* *3C 40*
    (off The Esplanade)
Berkeley M. PO19: Chich 2E 17
Bermuda Ct. BN17: L'ton 1H 35
Bernard Rd. BN18: Arun 5A 12
Berri Ct. BN18: Yap 6C 22
Berry Barn La. PO20: W Witt 3A 42
Berry Ct. PO19: Fish 1G 15
Berryfields PO21: Bers 3H 29
Berry La. BN17: L'ton 3G 35
    PO22: Bers .3H 29
Berrymill Cl. PO21: Bog R 1C 40
Bersted Grn. Ct. PO22: Bers 5B 30
Bersted M. PO22: Bog R 6C 30
Bersted St. PO22: Bog R 6B 30
    (not continuous)
Bethwines Cl. PO18: Fish 2F 15
Beverley Dr. BN18: Yap 6D 22
    PO20: Sel 4F 45
Beverley Gdns. BN16: Rust 1A 36
Bewick Gdns. PO19: Chich 1E 17
Bewley Rd. BN16: Ang 3E 27
Bickleys Ct. PO21: Bog R 3A 40
Bignor Cl. BN16: Rust 1C 36
BILSHAM 3C 32
Bilsham Cl. BN18: Yap 1C 32
Bilsham La. BN18: Bils 2A 32
Bilsham Rd. BN18: Bils, Yap 2C 32
BINSTED 6D 10
Binsted Av. PO22: Felp 6F 31
Binsted Ct. BN16: Rust 3A 36
Binsted La.
    BN18: Arun, Bins, Tort 5C 10
    BN18: Arun .6H 11
    PO21: Aldw .2E 39
Birch Cl. BN16: Ang 5E 27
Birches Cl. PO20: Sel 4C 44
Birdham Cl. PO21: Bers 6G 29

Birdham Rd. PO19: Apul, Chich 6H 15
  PO20: Bir, Donn, Apul 6H 15
Biscay Cl. BN17: L'ton 1A 36
Bishop Luffa Cl. PO19: Chich 2A 16
Bishops Cl. PO21: Pag 5B 38
Bishops Courtyard PO19: Chich 3E 17
  (off The Hornet)
Bishopsgate Wlk. PO19: Chich 2E 17
Bishop's Palace Garden 3C 16
Bishops Rd. PO20: Tang 5D 6
Blackberry Copse PO22: Felp 5G 31
Blackberry La. PO19: Chich 3F 17
  PO20: Sel 4C 44
Blackbird Way PO20: Sel 3E 45
Black Boy Ct. PO18: Fish 3F 15
Blackboy La. PO18: Fish 3F 15
Black Horse Caravan Pk. PO20: Sel 3C 44
  (off Mill La.)
Blackmill La. PO18: Eart, Nort 4B 8
Blacksmith Way PO22: Felp 5G 31
Blackthorn Av. PO22: Felp 5H 31
Blackwell Ct. PO21: Bers 4H 29
BLAKEHURST 5H 13
Blakehurst La. BN18: Poling, W'camp 5G 13
Blakehurst Way BN17: L'ton 1E 35
Blakemyle PO21: Aldw 3G 39
Blakeney Cl. PO19: Fish 3G 15
Blakes Rd. PO22: Felp 1F 41
Blakes Vw. PO22: Felp 1E 41
Blatchen, The BN17: L'ton 3G 35
Bleaches Ct. PO18: Mid L 1E 5
Blenheim Cl. BN16: Rust 6A 26
Blenheim Cl. PO21: Aldw 1F 39
Blenheim Dr. BN16: Rust 6A 26
Blenheim Gdns. PO19: Chich 3F 17
Blenheim Rd. BN18: Yap 1C 32
Blomfield Dr. PO19: Chich 6D 4
Blondel Dr. PO21: Aldw 2E 39
Bluebell Dr. BN17: L'ton 6H 25
Blue Cedars Cl. BN16: Ang 5D 26
Boardwalk PO19: Chich 2D 16
  (off Northgate)
Bognor Pier 3C 40
BOGNOR REGIS 2C 40
Bognor Regis Caravan Club Site PO22: Bers . .4C 30
Bognor Regis Golf Course 5F 31
Bognor Regis Mus. .3C 40
  (off Little High St.)
Bognor Regis Retail Pk. PO22: Bers 4C 30
Bognor Regis Station (Rail) 2B 40
Bognor Regis Town FC 2H 39
BOGNOR REGIS WAR MEMORIAL HOSPITAL . . .6B 30
Bognor Regis Wireless Mus. 3C 40
  (off Little High St.)
Bognor Rd. PO19: Chich 3F 17
  PO20: Oving 4G 17
Bognor Rd. Rdbt. PO19: Chich, Oving, Runc . .4G 17
Boleyn Dr. PO21: Pag 4C 38
Bond St. BN18: Arun 4B 12
Bonham Rd. PO21: Bers 4G 29
Bonnar Cl. PO20: Sel 5C 44
Bonnar Rd. PO20: Sel 5D 44
Bookers Cl. PO22: Bog R 6B 30
Bookers La. PO20: Earn 3H 43
BOSHAM 5A 14
Bosham La. PO18: Bosh 4A 14
Bosham Sailing Club 5A 14
Bosham Station (Rail) 2B 14
Bosham Walk 5A 14
Bostock Rd. PO19: Chich 1E 17
Botany Cl. BN16: Rust 3C 36
Boulevard, The PO20: Tang 5E 7
  PO21: Bers 4H 29
Boundary Way BN16: E Pres 1G 37
Bourne Cl. PO19: Fish 2F 15
Bourne Cl. BN17: Wick 6C 24
  (off Phoenix Cl.)
  PO20: E Witt 6F 43
Bowley La. PO20: S Mun 6A 28
Bowling Grn. Cl. PO21: Aldw 4C 38
BOXGROVE 4E 7
Boxgrove Gdns. PO21: Aldw 3D 38
Boxgrove Ho. PO18: Box 4E 7
Boxgrove Priory (remains) 4E 7
Box Tree Av. BN16: Rust 2A 36
BRACKLESHAM 6G 43
Bracklesham Bay Caravan & Boat Club
  PO20: Brac 6H 43
Bracklesham Cl. PO20: Brac 5G 43
Bracklesham La. PO20: Brac, E Witt 5G 43
Bradlond Cl. PO21: Aldw 3H 39
Bradshaw Rd. PO19: Chich 1F 17
Braemar Way PO21: Bers 4G 29
Bramber Cl. PO21: Bog R 1H 39
Bramber Rd. PO19: Chich 4E 17
Bramber Sq. BN16: Rust 1B 36
Bramble Cl. PO21: Pag 2A 38
Brambletyne Cl. BN16: Ang 3F 27
Bramblings, The BN16: Rust 2C 36
Bramfield Rd. PO22: Felp 1H 41
Bramley Gdns. PO22: Bers 4A 30
Bramley Way BN16: Ang 5F 27
Brampton Cl. PO20: Sel 4D 44

Brampton Ct. PO19: Chich 4C 16
  (off Stockbridge Rd.)
Brandy Hole La. PO19: Chich, W Bro 5B 4
Brazwick Av. PO21: Bers 4G 29
Bream Cl. BN17: Climp 3H 33
Bream La. PO20: Sel 3B 44
Brendon Way BN16: Rust 1A 36
Brent Rd. PO21: Bog R 1H 39
Brewery Hill BN18: Arun 4C 12
Briar Av. PO20: W Witt 2E 43
Briar Cl. BN16: Ang .5E 27
  BN18: Yap 6C 22
  PO20: Oving 3D 18
  PO21: Pag 2A 38
Briar Cott. Caravan Pk. PO20: E Witt 2F 43
Brickfield Cl. PO21: Bog R 6A 30
Brideoake Cl. PO19: Chich 1B 16
Bridger Cl. PO22: Felp 4F 31
Bridge Rd. BN17: L'ton 2C 34
  PO19: Chich 2E 17
Bridgeway, The PO20: Sel 5D 44
Bridle La. BN18: Slind 3A 10
Bridle Way, The PO20: Sel 4D 44
Bridorley Cl. PO21: Pag 3C 38
Brigham Pl. PO22: Felp 1H 41
Bristol Gdns. PO19: Chich 5C 4
Britannia Ct. Gdns. PO18: Bosh 4B 14
Britten's La. BN18: Eart, Font 4C 8
BROADBRIDGE 2B 14
Broadbridge Bus. Cen. PO18: Bosh 2A 14
Broadbridge Ct. PO18: Bosh 2B 14
Broadbridge Dr. PO18: Bosh 2B 14
Broadbridge Mill PO18: Bosh 2B 14
Broadmark Av. BN16: Rust 3B 36
Broadmark Beach BN16: Rust 4B 36
Broadmark Ho. BN16: Rust 2B 36
  (off Ash La.)
Broadmark La. BN16: Rust 4B 36
Broadmark Pde. BN16: Rust 2B 36
Broadmark Way BN16: Rust 3B 36
Broad Piece BN17: L'ton 1C 34
Broad Strand BN16: Rust 4C 36
Broad Vw. PO20: Sel 4F 45
Broadway PO20: Sel 3C 44
Broadway, The PO19: Chich 5C 4
Bronze Cl. PO22: Bers 4B 30
Brook Av. PO18: Bosh 4A 14
Brook Cl. PO21: Bog R 1H 39
Brookenbee Cl. BN16: Rust 6A 26
Brooklands PO21: Pag 4B 38
Brook La. BN16: Rust 6B 26
  PO22: Barn 6G 21
Brookpit La. BN17: Climp 3H 33
Brooks End PO21: Pag 3B 38
Brookside PO20: Runc 2A 28
Brookside Av. BN16: Rust 6B 26
Brookside Cl. PO20: Runc 2A 28
Brookside Ind. Est. BN16: Rust 6B 26
Brookside Pk. BN17: Lym 4D 24
Brooks La. PO18: Bosh 2C 14
  (not continuous)
  PO22: Bog R 6D 30
Brooks La. W. PO22: Bog R 6C 30
Brooksmead PO22: Bog R 1D 40
Broomcroft Rd. PO22: Felp 1H 41
Broomfield Rd. PO20: Sel 3F 45
Broom Fld. Way PO22: Felp 5F 31
Brou Cl. BN16: E Pres 2G 37
Broyle Cl. PO19: Chich 6C 4
Broyle Rd. PO19: Chich 6C 4
Brunswick Cl. PO22: Felp 6F 31
Buckingham Ct. PO22: Midd S 6B 32
Buckingham Dr. PO19: Chich 3G 17
Buckingham Pl. BN16: Rust 6A 26
Buckland Dr. PO21: Aldw 3C 38
Bucknor Cl. PO21: Aldw 3D 38
Bucksham Av. PO21: Bers 4G 29
Bulbeck Way PO22: Felp 5F 31
Burchett Wlk. PO21: Bers 6G 29
Burch Gro. BN18: Walb 6A 10
Burley Rd. PO22: Felp 1H 41
Burlington Gdns. PO20: Sel 5F 45
Burmill Ct. BN16: Rust 6D 26
BURNDELL 1E 33
Burndell Rd. BN18: Ford, Yap 6D 22
Burngreave Ct. PO21: Bog R 2A 40
Burnham Av. PO21: Bog R 2B 40
Burnham Gdns. PO21: Bog R 2B 40
Burns Gdns. PO22: Felp 5A 32
BURPHAM 1H 13
Bursledon Cl. PO22: Felp 6F 31
Burwash Ct. BN16: E Pres 6G 27
Bushby Av. BN16: Rust 2B 36
Butcher Cl. BN16: Ang 4F 27
Butlins Resort
  Bognor Regis 2D 40
Buttercup Gro. PO22: Felp 5G 31
Buttermere Way BN17: L'ton 6H 25
Butt La. BN18: Slind .1H 9
Butts, The BN17: Wick 5G 25
  (off Butts Mead)
Butts Mead BN17: Wick 5G 25

Bye Way, The PO21: Aldw 5D 38
Byeway, The PO20: W Witt 2B 42
Byfield Pl. PO22: Bers 5C 30
Byron Cl. PO22: Felp 5A 32
Byron Ct. PO19: Chich 5C 16
Byron Rd. BN16: Rust 2H 35
Bywater Way PO19: Chich 5C 16
Byway, The PO22: Midd S 6A 32
Byways PO20: Sel 6E 45

C

Caedwalla Dr. PO20: Tang 5D 6
Caen Stone Ct. BN18: Arun 5C 12
  (off Queen St.)
Caernarvon Rd. PO19: Chich 3G 17
Cakeham Rd. PO20: W Witt 2A 42
Cakeham Way PO20: W Witt 1A 42
Calceto La. BN17: Lym 1E 25
Caledon Av. PO22: Felp 6A 32
Caledonian Rd. PO19: Chich 3D 16
California M. BN18: Arun 5B 12
Cambrai Av. PO19: Chich 4E 17
Cambria Cl. PO18: Bosh 4B 14
Cambridge Av. PO20: W Witt 3D 42
Cambridge Dr. PO21: Aldw 1G 39
Cambridge Wlk. PO21: Aldw 1G 39
Camelia Cl. BN17: L'ton 6H 25
Campbell Dr. BN16: Rust 1A 36
Campbell Rd. PO20: Tang 6C 6
  PO21: Bog R 2C 40
Campion Cl. BN16: Rust 5A 26
Canada Gro. PO21: Bog R 2B 40
Canada Rd. BN18: Arun 4C 12
Canadian Cres. PO20: Sel 6E 45
Canal Pl. PO19: Chich 4C 16
Canal Rd. BN18: Yap 1C 32
Canal Wharf PO19: Chich 4C 16
Canal Wharf Rd. PO19: Chich 4C 16
Canberra Pl. PO20: Tang 5E 7
Canning Rd. PO22: Felp 2E 41
Canon La. PO19: Chich 3C 16
Canon's Cl. PO21: Aldw 4E 39
Canterbury Cl. PO19: Chich 1C 16
  PO21: Pag 4B 38
Canterbury Rd. BN16: Rust 1D 36
Canute Cl. PO20: Brac 6H 43
Canute Rd. PO18: Bosh 4A 14
Cape, The BN17: L'ton 2H 35
Capstan Dr. BN17: L'ton 6H 25
Cardinal's Dr. PO21: Pag 4B 38
Carina Dr. BN16: Ang 5E 27
Carleton Rd. PO19: Chich 1B 16
Carlingford Ct. PO21: Bog R 1B 40
Carlisle Gdns. PO19: Chich 6C 4
Carlton Av. PO21: Aldw 2D 38
Carnation Cl. BN17: L'ton 6A 26
Carnot Cl. PO21: Aldw 3H 39
Carousel Ct. PO22: Bog R 6A 30
Carse Rd. PO19: Chich 6F 5
Carvel Way BN17: L'ton 1H 35
Caspian Cl. PO18: Fish 1G 15
Cassells Rd. PO19: Chich 5D 4
Castle Gdns. BN18: Arun 4B 12
Castlereagh Grn. PO22: Felp 6F 31
Cathedral Cl. PO19: Chich 3C 16
  (off South St.)
Cathedral St. PO19: Chich 3D 16
  (off South St.)
Cathedral Way PO19: Chich 3A 16
Causeway, The BN18: Arun 5D 12
  PO20: Sel 3C 44
  PO21: Pag 5B 38
Causeway Cl. BN18: Arun 5D 12
Cavendish Ho. PO21: Bog R 3C 40
  (off Lennox St.)
Cavendish Rd. PO22: Bog R 2B 40
Cavendish St. PO19: Chich 2C 16
Cawley Rd. PO19: Chich 4D 16
Cedar Cl. BN16: Ang .5F 27
  PO21: Aldw 2E 39
Cedar Cl. E. PO21: Aldw 2F 39
Cedar Ct. PO19: Chich 5B 4
Cedar Lodge BN16: Rust 3B 36
  (off Cudlow Gdn.)
Cedars, The BN16: Rust 1D 36
  PO22: Barn 3G 21
Central Av. BN16: Rust 3B 36
Central Dr. PO21: Bers 5G 29
  PO22: Midd S 6D 32
Ceres Pl. PO22: Felp 6A 32
Chainbridge La. PO20: Brac 2B 44
Chalcraft La. PO21: Aldw, Bers, Lag 1F 39
Chalfont Cl. PO22: Midd S 6B 32
Challen Cl. PO20: Oving 3D 18
Chanctonbury Cl. BN16: Rust 3A 36
Chanctonbury Rd. BN16: Rust 3A 36
  (not continuous)
Chandler Rd. PO19: Chich 4B 16
Chandlers Lea PO20: Brac 6H 43
Channel Keep BN17: L'ton 3F 35

hannel Vw. PO21: Pag	5B 38
hantrelles, The BN16: Ang	4F 27
hantryfield Rd. BN16: Ang	3E 27
nantry Mead PO22: Barn	2F 21
hapel Cl. BN17: Wick	1D 34
hapel La. PO20: W Witt	1E 43
hapel St. PO19: Chich	2C 16
PO21: Bog R	2B 40
harles Av. PO19: Chich	3G 17
harlmead PO20: E Witt	5E 43
harlwood St. PO21: Bog R	3A 40
harnwood Rd. PO22: Bers	5A 30
harterhouse M. PO20: W Witt	3E 43
hase, The BN18: Font	4F 9
hatsworth Cl. BN16: Rust	6A 26
hatsworth Dr. BN16: Rust	6A 26
hatsworth Rd. PO19: Chich	6D 4
haucer Av. BN16: Rust	2A 36
haucer Dr. PO20: W Witt	3E 43
haucer Way PO22: Felp	5A 32
hawkmare Coppice	
PO21: Aldw	3F 39
hayle Gdns. PO20: Sel	5E 45
heal Ct. BN17: Wick	5G 25
(off Cheal Way)	
heal Way BN17: Wick	5F 25
heam Rd. BN16: Rust	3C 36
hequer La. PO18: Bosh	3C 14
hermont Ct. BN16: E Pres	1E 37
herry Av. BN18: Yap	1C 32
herry Cl. PO21: Aldw	3E 39
herry Cft. BN17: Wick	6E 25
herry Gdns. PO20: Sel	6D 44
herry Orchard Rd. PO19: Chich	4E 17
herry Tree Dr. PO20: E'gate	1E 21
heshire Cl. PO21: Bog R	1C 40
heshire Cres. PO22: Flan	4G 31
hessels Farm Dr. PO22: Flan	4G 31
hesswood Av. PO22: Felp	5H 31
hestnut Av. PO19: Chich	4C 4
hestnut Cl. BN16: Ang	5F 27
(Foxwood Av.)	
BN16: Ang	5E 27
(Sycamore Cl.)	
PO20: N Mun	5F 17
hestnut Ct. BN16: E Pres	2F 37
hestnut Gro. PO22: Bog R	5B 30
HESTNUT TREE HOUSE	
(CHILDREN'S HOSPICE)	1C 26
hestnut Wlk. PO20: Tang	6D 6
heveley Gdns. PO21: Aldw	3E 39
heviot Cl. BN16: E Pres	1F 37
HICHESTER	3D 16
hichester Bus. Pk. PO20: Tang	5E 7
hichester By-Pass	
PO19: Chich, Westh, Oving	1G 17
hichester Cathedral	3C 16
HICHESTER CENTRE, THE	1E 17
hichester Ct. BN16: Rust	1B 36
hichester Crematorium PO19: Chich	1F 17
hichester Dr. PO20: Tang	6D 6
hichester Festival Theatre	1D 16
hichester Food Pk. PO20: Runc	6A 18
hichester Ga. PO19: Chich	4C 16
hichester Minerva Theatre	2D 16
HICHESTER NUFFIELD HEALTH HOSPITAL	6C 4
hichester Rd. BN18: Arun	4F 11
PO20: Sel	3E 45
PO20: W Witt	1D 42
PO21: Bers, Bog R	3F 29
hichester Station (Rail)	4C 16
hichester Way PO20: Sel	3G 45
hilgrove Pl. BN18: Yap	1D 32
hiltern Cl. BN16: E Pres	1F 37
hine, The BN17: L'ton	3H 35
hipley Ct. PO21: Bog R	1H 39
hristchurch Cres. PO21: Aldw	2F 39
hristie Pl. PO22: Bers	5C 30
hurch App. BN17: L'ton	2F 35
hurch Cl. PO21: Pag	6A 38
hurch Farm Ct. PO20: E Witt	3F 43
hurch Farm Holiday Village PO21: Pag	6A 38
hurch Farm La. PO20: E Witt	3F 43
hurchfields BN16: E Pres	1E 37
hurch Hill BN16: Ang	4E 27
BN18: Slind	2H 9
hurch Ho. M. PO22: Felp	1F 41
(off Felpham Rd.)	
hurchill Av. PO21: Aldw	1F 39
hurchill Ho. PO22: Barn	4H 21
hurchill Pde. BN16: Rust	2B 36
hurchill Wlk. PO21: Pag	5B 38
(off Ashcroft Way)	
hurch La. BN17: Climp	2H 33
BN17: Lym	3D 24
BN18: Walb	1B 22
BN18: Yap	5C 22
PO18: Box	4E 7
PO20: E'gate	2D 20
PO20: Oving	2D 18
PO20: Tang	6D 6
PO21: Pag	5A 38
Church La. PO22: Barn	5G 21
PO22: Bog R	6B 30
Churchmead Cl. PO18: Mid L	1C 4
Church Mdw. PO18: Bosh	4A 14
Church Path PO21: Bog R	1C 40
PO22: Midd S	6C 32
Church Rd. BN16: Ang	4E 27
BN16: Rust	2B 36
BN18: Yap	6C 22
PO19: Chich	1F 17
PO20: Ald	1H 19
PO20: E Witt	4E 43
PO20: Sel	3E 45
Churchside PO19: Chich	3C 16
Church Sq. PO19: Chich	3D 16
Church St. BN17: L'ton	2F 35
Church Way PO21: Pag	4B 38
Churchwood Dr. PO20: Tang	6E 7
Churt Dr. PO22: Bers	5C 30
Cinders La. BN18: Yap	1D 32
Cineworld Cinema	
Chichester	4C 16
Circle, The BN16: E Pres	3F 37
City Bus. Cen. PO19: Chich	4C 16
(off Basin Rd.)	
City Flds. Bus. Pk. PO20: Tang	5E 7
City Flds. Way PO20: Tang	5E 7
Claigmar Rd. BN16: Rust	2B 36
Clappers La. PO20: Brac, Earn	5G 43
Clare Lodge BN16: Rust	2A 36
(off Sea La.)	
Claremont Cl. BN16: Ang	3E 27
Claremont Ct. PO21: Bog R	2C 40
(off Campbell Rd.)	
Claremont Gdns. PO20: E'gate	5E 9
Clarence Av. BN17: Wick	6D 24
Clarence Dr. BN16: E Pres	1E 37
Clarence Ga. PO21: Bog R	2C 40
(off High St.)	
Clarence Rd. PO21: Bog R	2C 40
Claridge Ho. BN17: L'ton	2F 35
Clay La. BN18: Cross, W'camp	6G 13
PO18: W Ash, E Ash, Fish	1E 15
PO19: Chich, Fish	1G 15
Claypit La. PO18: Good, Westh	3H 5
Clayton Cl. PO20: Sel	5C 44
Clayton La. PO20: Brac	5C 44
Clayton Rd. PO20: Sel	5C 44
Cleeves Ct. BN16: Rust	1D 36
Cleeves Way BN16: Rust	1D 36
Cleveland Rd. PO19: Chich	4E 17
Clevets, The PO21: Aldw	4D 38
Clifton Ct. PO21: Bog R	2B 40
(off Clifton Rd.)	
Clifton Rd. BN17: L'ton	3E 35
PO21: Bog R	1B 40
CLIMPING	2A 34
Climping Pk. BN17: L'ton	2A 34
Climping St. BN17: Climp	3G 33
Clock Pk. PO22: Bers	5D 30
Cloisters, The BN17: L'ton	3C 16
CLOSE, THE	3C 16
Close, The BN16: Rust	3C 36
PO18: Box	4E 7
PO18: Mid L	2C 4
PO19: Chich	3C 16
PO20: Sel	4D 44
PO21: Aldw	4D 38
PO22: Midd S	6D 32
Clovelly Av. PO22: Felp	6G 31
Clover Mead PO22: Felp	5H 31
Club Wlk. BN16: E Pres	3F 37
Clun Rd. BN17: L'ton, Wick	6C 24
Clydesdale Av. PO19: Chich	4D 16
Clydesdale Gdns. PO22: Bers	4H 29
Coach Ho. Cl. BN16: Rust	1D 36
PO20: Sel	4E 45
Coach Rd. PO18: Westh	6H 5
PO20: Oving	1A 18
Coastal Rd. BN16: E Pres, King G	3G 37
Coastguard La. PO20: W Witt	2A 42
Coastguard Pde. PO21: Aldw	4E 39
(off Barrack La.)	
Coastguard Rd. BN17: L'ton	4E 35
(off Arun Pde.)	
Coastguards Cotts. PO20: W Witt	1A 42
Cobham Cl. BN18: Yap	1C 32
Cohen Cl. PO20: Ald	4C 20
Coldicott M. PO22: Midd S	6D 32
Colebrook Rd. BN17: Wick	6D 24
College Cl. PO21: Aldw	1G 39
College La. PO19: Chich	6D 4
Collins Cl. PO20: E'gate	1E 21
Collyer Av. PO21: Bers, Bog R	6H 29
Colt's Bay PO21: Aldw	4D 38
Colt St. PO20: Sel	3D 44
Columbine Way BN17: L'ton	6A 26
COLWORTH	1F 29
Colworth Rd. PO21: Bers	3G 29
Combined Court Cen.	
Chichester	4D 16
Commonmead La. PO21: Pag	2B 38
Compass Cl. BN17: L'ton	1H 35
Compton Cl. PO19: Chich	4D 4
Compton Ct. BN16: Rust	1B 36
Compton Dr. PO22: Felp	5A 32
Conbar Av. BN16: Rust	1B 36
Condor M. BN17: Wick	5D 24
(off Kestrel Way)	
Conduit Mead PO19: Chich	1F 17
Coney Cl. PO20: E Witt	5E 43
Coney Rd. PO20: E Witt	5E 43
Coney Six PO20: E Witt	5E 43
Conifer Way PO21: Pag	3A 38
Coniston Cl. PO22: Felp	5G 31
Coniston Way BN17: L'ton	6H 25
Connaught Ho. PO21: Bog R	3B 40
(off The Esplanade)	
Connaught Rd. BN17: L'ton	2E 35
Connolly Way PO19: Chich	6D 4
Constable Dr. PO20: Sel	4F 45
Conway Dr. PO21: Pag	5B 38
Coombe La. BN18: Burp	1H 13
Coomes Way BN17: Wick	5E 25
Coopers Farm Cl. PO22: Bog R	6C 30
Cooper St. PO20: Sel	3D 16
Cootes La. PO22: Midd S	6C 32
Copeland Rd. PO22: Felp	1F 41
Copper Beech Dr. PO20: Tang	6D 6
Copper Hall Cl. BN16: Rust	1D 36
Coppets Wood BN16: Rust	3A 36
Coppice, The BN16: Rust	1C 36
Coppice La. PO20: Sel	3D 44
Copse, The PO19: Chich	5D 4
Copse La. BN18: Walb	5A 10
Copse Vw. BN16: E Pres	1E 37
Copthorne Caravan Site PO21: Aldw	1E 39
Copthorne Way PO21: Aldw	1E 39
Coral Cl. PO20: Sel	3B 44
Coral La. PO20: Sel	3B 44
Corbishley Grn. PO22: Bog R	5B 30
Corbishley Rd. PO22: Bog R	5B 30
Cordal Cl. BN16: Rust	4A 36
Cormorant Way PO20: E Witt	5F 43
Corner Ho. PO20: E'gate	2E 21
Cornfield Cl. BN17: Wick	6F 25
Cornfields, The PO20: Westg	2C 20
Cornflower Cl. PO19: Chich	1F 17
(off Story Rd.)	
Cornwall Gdns. BN17: L'ton	1E 35
Cornwall Rd. BN17: L'ton	1E 35
Cory Cl. PO19: Chich	4D 16
Cosens Way PO22: Felp	5G 31
Cotland Rd. PO20: Sel	5F 45
Cotswold Way BN16: E Pres	1F 37
Cottage Cl. PO21: Aldw	3D 38
Cottrell Cl. BN16: Ang	4E 27
Cottrells, The BN16: Ang	4E 27
Countisbury Cl. PO21: Aldw	2G 39
Court, The PO21: Pag	4B 38
Courtfield Ho. PO21: Bog R	2A 40
(off Hambledon Pl.)	
Courtlands Way PO22: Felp	5H 31
Courtwick La. BN17: Wick	5C 24
Courtwick Rd. BN17: Wick	6D 24
Coventry Cl. PO21: Aldw	1E 39
Cove Rd. BN16: Rust	3A 36
Cowdray Cl. BN16: Rust	6A 26
Cowdray Dr. BN16: Rust	6A 26
Cowdray Wlk. BN16: Rust	6A 26
(off Cowdray Dr.)	
Cowslip Gdns. PO22: Felp	5G 31
Coxes Rd. PO20: Sel	5C 44
Coxswain Way PO20: Sel	6E 45
Crablands PO20: Sel	4C 44
Crablands Cl. PO20: Sel	4C 44
Crab Tree Cl. BN17: Wick	4E 25
Craigweil La. PO21: Aldw	3F 39
Craigweil Mnr. PO21: Aldw	4E 39
Crane St. PO19: Chich	3D 16
Cranford Gdns. PO21: Bog R	1B 40
Crede Cl. PO18: Bosh	4B 14
Crede La. PO18: Bosh	3B 14
Creek End PO19: Fish	3G 15
Crescent, The BN16: E Pres	3F 37
BN16: Rust	3H 35
PO20: W Witt	4D 42
PO21: Pag	5B 38
PO22: Felp	1F 41
Crescenta Wlk. PO21: Bog R	2H 39
Crescent Rd. PO21: Bog R	2B 40
Cressey Way PO19: Chich	6D 4
Crimsham Rd. PO22: Bers	4H 29
Critchfield Rd. PO18: Bosh	4A 14
Critchmere Rd. PO20: E'gate	2E 21
Croft, The BN16: E Pres	2F 37
BN18: Yap	5C 22
PO21: Bers	6G 29
Croftcost La. PO22: Felp	5A 32
Croft Mead PO19: Chich	5D 4
Croft Rd. PO20: Sel	5D 44
Croft Way PO20: Sel	4D 44
PO21: Pag	5H 31
Crookthorn La. BN17: Climp	3G 33

Cropthorne Dr. BN17: Climp 2H 33
Crosbie Cl. PO19: Chich 6C 16
CROSSBUSH 6E 13
Crossbush By-Pass BN18: Cross, Poling . .1F 25
Crossbush La. BN18: Cross, Poling 6E 13
Crossbush Rd. PO22: Felp 1G 41
Crosshaven BN17: L'ton 1H 35
Cross Rd. BN16: Rust 2D 36
Crossways BN16: E Pres 6G 27
    PO22: Midd S 6C 32
Crossways, The BN17: Wick 6D 24
Crouch Cross La. PO18: Box 4D 6
Crown Yd. M. BN18: Arun 4C 12
    (off River Rd.)
Croy Cl. PO19: Chich 5B 16
Crundens Cnr. BN16: Rust 1D 36
Cuckoo Flds. PO18: Fish 1G 15
Cudlow Av. BN16: Rust 2B 36
Cudlow Gdn. BN16: Rust 2B 36
    (not continuous)
Culimore Cl. PO20: W Witt 4D 42
Culimore Rd. PO20: W Witt 4D 42
Cullum Cl. PO19: Chich 1F 17
Culver Rd. PO22: Felp 1F 41
Cumberland Cl. BN16: Ang 4F 27
Cumberland Cres. BN16: Ang 4E 27
Cumberland Rd. BN16: Ang 4F 27
Cunliffe Cl. PO20: W Witt 1B 42
Cunningham Gdns. PO22: Felp 6H 31
Curlescroft PO21: Aldw 3G 39
Cutfield Cl. PO19: Chich 6C 16
Cutten Way PO19: Chich 3E 17
Cygnet Wlk. PO22: Bers 5A 30
Cypress Way PO21: Aldw 3E 39

D

Dairy La. BN18: Walb 6A 10
    PO18: Westh 6A 6
Daisy Flds. Touring Pk. BN17: Wick 6F 25
Dale Way PO22: Felp 5G 31
Dallaway Rd. PO19: Chich 5E 17
Dalloway Rd. BN18: Arun 5H 11
Daltons Pl. BN18: Arun 5B 12
Dame School Ct. PO18: E Lav 1D 4
Danefield Rd. PO20: Sel 5C 44
Dapper's La. BN16: Ang 3F 27
Dark La. PO21: Aldw 3F 39
Darlington Cl. BN16: Ang 4F 27
Darlingtons, The BN16: Rust 6D 26
Darlington Wlk. BN16: Rust 6D 26
    (off The Leas)
Davenport Rd. PO22: Felp 1F 41
Davids Cl. PO21: Bers 6G 29
Davits Dr. BN17: L'ton 1H 35
Dawtrey Cl. BN16: Rust 1D 36
Days La. BN18: Font 4E 9
Dean BN17: Wick 6D 24
Deanery Cl. PO19: Chich 3C 16
Deanery Farm La. PO19: Chich 3C 16
    (off Southgate)
Deanery Sq. PO21: Bers 4G 29
Deans Cl. BN18: Font 4F 9
Decoy Dr. BN16: Ang 2E 27
Decoy La. BN18: Poling 2C 26
    PO20: Tang .2G 19
Deepdene Cl. PO22: Midd S 6D 32
Deer Cl. PO19: Apul 6B 16
Deer Pk. Cl. PO20: Sel 3B 44
Deer Pk. Dr. PO20: Sel 3B 44
Deer Pk. La. PO20: Sel 3A 44
Deeside Av. PO19: Fish 2G 15
Defiance Pl. PO22: Felp 1H 41
Dell, The PO22: Bers 5H 29
Dell Dr. BN16: Ang 5E 27
Delling Dr. PO18: Bosh 3A 14
Delling La. PO18: Bosh 4B 14
Dempsey Rd. PO19: Chich 5D 4
Den Av. PO21: Bog R 2C 40
Denge La. PO18: Hal 1F 7
Denham Cl. PO22: Midd S 6B 32
Denmans Gdns. .4E 9
Denmans La. BN18: Font 5D 8
    PO20: Font .5D 8
Denny's Cl. PO20: Sel 4E 45
Denshare Rd. PO20: Sel 3E 45
Densihale PO21: Aldw 2H 39
Derwent Cl. BN17: L'ton 1H 35
    PO20: Tang .5E 7
Derwent Gro. PO22: Felp 5G 31
Devonshire Pl. PO21: Bog R 2B 40
Devonshire Rd. PO21: Bog R 2A 40
Dial Cl. PO22: Barn 4H 21
Dickinson Pl. PO22: Bers 5C 30
Dingley Rd. PO19: Fish 2A 36
Dinsdale Fld. BN16: Rust 6D 26
Dinsdale Gdns. BN16: Rust 1B 36
Ditchfield Cl. PO22: Felp 5A 32
Dolphin Cl. PO19: Fish 3G 15
Dolphin Ct. BN16: Rust 3C 36
    PO21: Bog R .3B 40
    (off The Steyne)

Dolphin M. PO19: Chich 3A 16
Dolphin Way BN16: Rust 3C 36
Domehouse Cl. PO20: Sel 6E 45
Dominican Friary (remains of) 4D 12
Dominion Way BN16: Rust 6B 26
Donaldson Cl. PO20: Sel 3C 44
Donegal Rd. PO19: Chich 6D 4
Donnington Pk. PO20: Apul 6A 16
Donnington Pl. BN16: Rust 1B 36
    (off Woodlands Av.)
Dorset Cl. BN17: L'ton 1F 35
Dorset Rd. PO21: Bog R 6B 30
Douglas Cl. BN18: Ford 1E 33
    PO22: Midd S 6C 32
Douglas Martin Rd. PO19: Chich 2E 17
Dove Ct. PO22: Bers 5A 30
Dover La. BN16: Poling, W'camp, Ang 1C 26
Downing Cl. PO21: Aldw 1F 39
Downland Cl. PO19: Chich 1C 16
Downlands Cl. PO21: Pag 3B 38
Downs Way BN16: Ang 6E 27
Downview Cl. BN18: Yap 6D 22
    PO18: Mid L .1B 4
    PO20: E Witt .5F 43
Downview Rd. BN18: Yap 6D 22
    PO22: Barn 2F 21
    PO22: Bers 6F 31
Downview Way BN18: Yap 6D 22
DRAYTON 3B 18
Drayton La. PO20: Oving 2A 18
Drewetts Cl. BN16: Rust 6A 26
Drewitts M. PO20: Oving 2D 18
Drift La. PO20: Sel 3C 44
Drift Rd. PO20: Sel 2F 45
    PO21: Aldw, Pag 3C 38
Driftway, The BN16: Rust 1A 36
Drills, The BN16: Ang 4E 27
    (off High St.)
Drive, The BN16: E Pres 3G 37
    PO18: Bosh .4B 14
    PO18: Westh .5H 5
    PO19: Chich 4C 4
    PO20: E'gate .6F 9
    PO21: Aldw 4E 39
Drove La. BN18: Yap 2H 31
    PO20: Earn 5H 43
Drovers Way PO22: Barn 3F 21
Dryad Way PO22: Felp 6A 32
Drygrounds La. PO22: Felp 6E 31
Duck La. PO20: Sel 3B 44
Dukes Cl. BN18: Arun 5A 12
Dukes Ct. BN17: L'ton 2E 35
    PO19: Chich .4G 17
Dukes Mdw. PO21: Pag 2C 38
Duke's Rd. BN18: Font 2D 8
Duke St. BN17: L'ton 2E 35
Duncan Rd. PO19: Chich 1C 16
Duncton Cl. PO22: Felp 1G 41
Duncton Rd. BN16: Rust 5A 26
Dunes, The PO21: Aldw 5D 38
Dunstan Cl. PO19: Chich 4D 4
Durban Pk. PO22: Bers 6C 30
Durban Pk. Ind. Est. PO22: Bers 5C 30
Durban Rd. PO22: Bers 5B 30
Durban Rd. Bus. Cen. PO22: Bers 5C 30
Durham Cl. PO21: Pag 5B 38
Durham Gdns. PO19: Chich 6C 4
Durlston Dr. PO22: Bers, Bog R 5A 30
Durlston Pde. PO22: Bers 5A 30
Durnford Cl. PO19: Chich 2B 16
Duxford Cl. PO20: Tang 5D 6
Dyers La. BN18: Slind 2H 9

E

Eagles Chase BN17: Wick 5E 25
EARNLEY 4H 43
Earnley Mnr. Cl. PO20: Earn 4H 43
Earnley Pl. PO20: Earn 4H 43
East Av. PO22: Midd S 5C 32
East Bank BN18: Yap 4D 22
    PO20: Sel 4F 45
E. Bank Wlk. BN17: L'ton 3H 35
    (off Ketch Rd.)
EAST BEACH 3F 45
E. Beach Rd. PO20: Sel 3G 45
E. Bracklesham Dr. PO20: Brac 6G 43
East Cl. PO22: Midd S 6B 32
East Ct. Way BN16: Rust 1D 36
East Dr. BN16: Ang 5D 26
    PO22: Midd S 6D 32
EASTERGATE 2E 21
Eastergate Grn. BN16: Rust 2B 36
Eastergate Ho. PO20: E'gate 2D 20
Eastergate La. BN18: Walb 6E 9
    PO20: E'gate .6E 9
Eastern Cl. BN16: E Pres 1G 37
E. Front Rd. PO21: Pag 6B 38
Eastgate Ct. PO19: Chich 3E 17
    (off The Hornet)

Eastgate Sq. PO19: Chich 3D 16
EAST HAMPNETT 5F
Easthampnett Caravan Pk. PO18: Tang . . .5G
Easthampnett La. PO18: Tang 5F
East Ham Rd. BN17: L'ton 2D 3
EAST KINGSTON 2H 3
East Lake PO21: Bog R 1C 4
Eastland Rd. PO19: Chich 5E 1
EAST LAVANT 2D
East Mead PO21: Pag 5B 3
Eastmead Ind. Est. PO18: Mid L 1E
Eastover Way PO22: Felp 5H 3
East Pallant PO19: Chich 3D 1
Eastpoint PO20: Sel 3E 4
EAST PRESTON .2F 3
East Row PO19: Chich 3D 1
East Strand PO20: W Witt 3A 4
East St. BN17: L'ton 2E 3
    PO19: Chich .3D 1
    PO20: Sel 4D 4
East Vw. Cl. PO18: Mid L 1F
East Wlk. BN16: E Pres 3E 3
East Walls PO19: Chich 3D 1
E. Walls Cl. PO19: Chich 3D 1
    (off East Walls
East Way PO20: Sel 4F 4
EAST WITTERING 4E 4
E. Wittering Bus. Cen. PO20: E Witt 3F 4
Ecclesden La. BN16: Ang 4G 2
Eden Ct. BN17: Wick 5G 2
    (off Gratwicke Dr.
Edinburgh Cl. PO21: Aldw 3F 3
Edwards Av. PO20: Tang 5D
Edwards Way BN17: Wick 5D 2
Edwen Cl. PO21: Pag 2C 3
Edwin Cl. PO21: Bers 4H 2
Eels Cross PO20: Sel 3B 4
Egan Way BN17: Wick 1C 3
ELBRIDGE 2F 2
Elbridge Av. PO21: Bers 4G 2
Elbridge Cres. PO21: Aldw 3D 3
Elbridge Sq. PO21: Bers 3H 2
Elcombe Cl. PO20: Brac 6G 4
Eldon Way BN17: Wick 6C 2
Eleanor Gdns. PO22: Felp 6A 3
Elfin Gro. PO21: Bog R 2A 4
Elfin M. PO21: Bog R 2A 4
Elgin Cl. PO19: Chich 4D 1
    (off Stirling Rd.
Elizabeth Av. PO21: Aldw 1D 3
Elizabeth Cl. PO20: Sel 2D 3
Elizabeth Ct. PO21: Bog R 3A 4
    (off Park Ter
Elizabeth Rd. PO19: Chich 2G 1
Ella Cl. PO20: W Witt 4D 4
Ellanore La. PO20: W Witt 1A 4
Ellasdale Rd. PO21: Bog R 2A 4
Ella Ter. BN18: Poling 1B 2
Ellis Cl. BN18: Arun 5A 1
Ellis Sq. PO20: Sel 2F 4
Ellis Way PO21: Pag 5B 3
Elm Av. BN16: E Pres 2G 3
Elm Cl. PO20: Brac 5G 4
    PO21: Pag 4B 3
Elmcroft Pl. PO20: Westg 3C 2
Elm Dale PO22: Barn 3F 2
Elmdene Ct. PO20: Brac 6G 4
Elm Dr. PO22: Midd S 6E 3
ELMER 6E 3
Elmer Cl. PO22: Midd S 6E 3
Elmer Ct. PO22: Midd S 5D 3
Elmer Rd. PO22: Midd S 6C 3
Elm Gro. PO20: Sel 4D 4
    PO21: Bog R .2H 3
    PO22: Barn 2F 2
Elm Gro. Rd. BN17: L'ton 1F 3
Elm Gro. Sth. PO22: Barn 3F 2
Elmhurst Cl. BN16: Ang 3F 2
Elm Pk. PO18: Bosh 3B 1
Elm Pl. BN16: Rust 1C 3
Elm Rd. PO20: Westg 2D 2
Elmsfield PO20: Sel 4E 4
Elms La. PO20: W Witt 2B 4
Elms Ride PO20: W Witt 2B 4
Elmstead Gdns. PO20: W Witt 1B 4
Elmstead Pk. Rd. PO20: W Witt 1B 4
Elms Way PO20: W Witt 1B 4
Elm Tree Cl. PO20: Sel 3E 4
    PO21: Bers 5H 2
Elmwood Av. PO22: Bog R 6C 3
Elsaw Cl. PO19: Chich 4D 1
Elspring Mead BN17: Wick 6D 2
Ely Cl. PO20: W Witt 3D 4
Ely Gdns. PO21: Aldw 2E 3
Emmabrook Ct. BN16: Rust 4H 3
    (off Sea Rd
Empress Cl. BN17: Wick 5E 2
Ensign Way BN17: L'ton 1H 3
Enterprise Units PO22: Bers 5C 3
Epsom Gdns. BN16: Rust 1D 3
Esher Cl. PO21: Pag 3C 3
Esher Dr. BN17: L'ton 2G 3
Esmonde Cl. BN17: L'ton 3G 3

lanade, The PO21: Bog R	.3B 40
PO22: Felp	.2E 41
sex Rd. PO21: Bog R	.6B 30
uary, The BN17: L'ton	.2G 35
n Cl. PO21: Aldw	.1F 39
n Dr. PO20: W Witt	.3E 43
rick Cl. PO19: Chich	.4E 17
rick Rd. PO19: Chich	.4D 16
elyn Av. BN16: Rust	.3C 36
ans Pl. PO22: Bers	.5C 30
ens Gdns. PO22: Barn	.2F 21
eter Cl. PO21: Aldw	.2G 39
eter Rd. PO19: Chich	.6B 4
on Rd. PO19: Chich	.5D 16

F

irfield Cl. PO18: Bosh	.4B 14
irfield Rd. PO18: Bosh	.4A 14
irholme Dr. BN18: Yap	.1D 32
irlands BN16: E Pres	.2E 37
PO22: Bers	.5H 29
irlawn BN16: Rust	.1B 36
irlead BN17: L'ton	.3G 35
irlight Ct. BN17: L'ton	.3E 35
irmile Bottom BN18: Made	.1D 10
irway BN17: L'ton	.3G 35
irway, The PO21: Aldw	.5C 38
icon Gdns. BN17: Wick	.5D 24
ikland Av. BN17: L'ton	.1G 35
iklands Cl. PO22: Bog R	.6C 30
resmead PO21: Aldw	.3G 39
rm Acre BN16: E Pres	.1E 37
rm Cl. PO18: Fish	.3F 15
PO22: Midd S	.6E 33
rm Cnr. PO22: Midd S	.6D 32
rm Rd. PO20: Brac	.6G 43
rm Way BN16: Rust	.2A 36
rndell Cl. PO19: Chich	.2F 17
rnhurst Rd. PO22: Barn	.3G 21
roes, The BN17: L'ton	.1H 35
stnet Way BN17: L'ton	.1H 35
tting Ground La. PO22: Barn	.6F 21
ulkner Gdns. BN17: Wick	.6F 25
ellows Gdns. BN18: Yap	.1D 32
ELPHAM	.1G 41
elpham Gdns. PO22: Felp	.6G 31
elpham Rd. PO22: Felp	.2E 41
elpham Way PO22: Bog R, Felp	.1D 40
erndale Rd. PO19: Chich	.5D 4
erndale Wlk. BN16: Ang	.3F 27
erndown Gdns. PO22: Felp	.6F 31
ernhurst Gdns. PO21: Aldw	.3E 39
ernleigh Cl. PO19: Chich	.3H 15
erring Gdns. PO22: Felp	.6F 31
erry Rd. BN17: L'ton	.3B 34
estival Ct. PO19: Chich	.2D 16
(off Somerstown)	
ncham Cl. BN16: E Pres	.2E 37
eld Cl. BN18: Walb	.6A 10
eld Ho. BN16: E Pres	.1E 37
eld Pl. BN17: L'ton	.2E 35
eld Rd. PO20: E Witt	.4F 43
elds, The PO20: Westg	.2C 20
(off Meadow Way)	
inisterre Way BN17: L'ton	.3H 35
ircroft Cres. BN16: Rust	.1C 36
rs Av. PO22: Felp	.6G 31
rs Av. W. PO22: Felp	.6G 31
rst Av. PO20: Brac	.6G 43
PO22: Felp	.1G 41
PO22: Midd S	.5B 32
rtree Cl. PO20: N Mun	.5G 17
r Tree Way PO22: Bers	.4B 30
ISHBOURNE	.2G 15
ishbourne Rd. (East) PO19: Chich	.3H 15
ishbourne Rd. (West) PO19: Fish	.3G 15
ishbourne Roman Palace & Gardens	.3G 15
ishbourne Rdbt. PO19: Chich	.4A 16
ishbourne Station (Rail)	.2F 15
ishermans Quay BN17: L'ton	.3E 35
(off Surrey St.)	
ishermans Wlk. PO20: Sel	.5F 45
PO21: Aldw	.4E 39
ishers Cl. BN17: L'ton	.3H 35
ish La. PO20: Sel	.3B 44
PO21: Aldw	.3G 39
itness First	
Bognor Regis	.4C 30
ittleworth Dr. PO22: Felp	.5H 31
ittleworth Gdn. BN16: Rust	.2B 36
itzalan Ct. BN16: Rust	.4A 36
(off Rackham Rd.)	
itzalan M. BN18: Arun	.5C 12
itzalan Rd. BN17: L'ton	.3F 35
BN18: Arun	.6B 12
(not continuous)	
itzleet Ho. PO21: Bog R	.2B 40

Fitzroy Ct. BN17: L'ton	.2F 35
Fitzwilliam Cl. PO21: Aldw	.1G 39
FLANSHAM	.4G 31
Flansham Bus. Cen. PO22: Flan	.4G 31
Flansham La. PO22: Felp	.6H 31
Flansham M. PO22: Felp	.5H 31
Flansham Pk. PO22: Felp	.5H 31
Flaxman Av. PO19: Chich	.3A 16
Flax Mean PO22: Felp	.6G 31
Flax Mean Ho. PO22: Felp	.6G 31
Fleet Cl. BN17: L'ton	.1H 35
Fleming Ct. PO21: Pag	.4B 38
Fletcher Cl. PO21: Pag	.3C 38
Fletcher Way BN16: Ang	.3E 27
PO21: Bog R	.6A 30
Flint Cl. BN16: E Pres	.1E 37
Flora Ct. BN17: Wick	.6C 24
(off Phoenix Cl.)	
Florence Rd. PO19: Chich	.3F 17
Follett Cl. PO21: Aldw	.4F 39
Follis Gdns. PO19: Fish	.2G 15
FONTWELL	.4F 9
Fontwell Av.	
BN18: Font, Slind, Walb	.1D 20
PO20: E'gate, Font	.1D 20
Fontwell Cl. BN16: Rust	.3A 36
BN18: Font	.5F 9
Fontwell Rd. PO20: Sel	.3G 45
Fontwell Park Racecourse	.5E 9
Forbes Pl. PO19: Chich	.1C 16
FORD	.5H 23
Ford Airfield Ind. Est. BN18: Ford	.6E 23
Fordingbridge Ind. Site PO22: Barn	.2F 21
Ford La. BN18: Ford, Yap	.5D 22
Ford La. Bus. Pk. BN18: Ford	.5G 23
Ford Rd. BN18: Arun, Ford, Sort	.4H 23
BN18: Climp, Ford	.6H 23
Ford Station (Rail)	.4H 23
Fordwater Gdns. BN18: Ford	.1E 33
Fordwater La. PO19: Chich	.5D 4
Fordwater Rd. PO18: E Lav	.2D 4
PO19: Chich	.5D 4
Forge, The PO20: Sel	.4D 44
Forge Cl. BN16: E Pres	.1E 37
PO19: Chich	.6B 16
Forsters Yd. BN17: L'ton	.2C 34
Fort Rd. BN17: L'ton, Wick	.1C 34
Fort Rd. E. BN17: Wick	.1D 34
Fort Rd. Ind. Est. BN17: L'ton	.1C 34
Fosters BN16: E Pres	.3D 36
Fosters Cl. BN16: E Pres	.3D 36
Foundry Rd. BN18: Yap	.6C 22
Fourteen Acre Av. PO22: Felp	.5G 31
Fourth Av. PO22: Felp	.1H 41
Fox Cl. PO19: Chich	.1F 17
Foxdale Dr. BN16: Ang	.5E 27
Foxes Cl. BN16: Rust	.5A 26
Foxes Cft. PO22: Barn	.3H 21
Foxglove Way BN17: L'ton	.6H 25
Foxwarren Cl. PO20: W Witt	.4E 43
Foxwood Av. BN16: Ang	.5F 27
Frampton Cl. PO19: Fish	.2F 15
Framptons, The BN16: E Pres	.2G 37
France La. BN13: Pat	.1H 27
Franciscan Way BN17: L'ton	.2E 35
Francis Ct. BN17: L'ton	.2F 35
Frandor Rd. PO21: L'ton	.6G 29
Frankalan M. PO21: Bog R	.3B 40
Franklin Pl. PO19: Chich	.2D 16
Fraser Cl. PO20: Sel	.5F 45
Fraser Row PO18: Fish	.1G 15
Frederick Rd. PO19: Chich	.3H 15
Freeland Cl. PO19: Chich	.3H 15
Freeman Cl. BN18: Walb	.6G 9
Freeways PO20: Sel	.3C 44
Freeways Caravan Site PO20: Sel	.3C 44
Frensham Av. PO22: Bers	.5C 30
Freya Cl. PO22: Midd S	.6C 32
Friary Cl. PO22: Midd S	.6C 32
Friary La. PO19: Chich	.3D 16
Frith Rd. PO21: Bog R	.1H 39
Frobisher Rd. PO21: Aldw	.3D 38
Frobisher Way BN16: Rust	.3D 36
Fullers Wlk. BN17: Wick	.4E 25
Fulmar Way PO20: Tang	.6F 7
Furlong Cl. BN18: Walb	.4G 9
Furse Feld PO21: Aldw	.3H 39
Furze Cl. PO18: Westh	.6H 5
Furzedown BN17: L'ton	.3F 35
Furzefield PO20: W Witt	.2E 43
Furzefield Cl. BN16: Ang	.2E 27

G

Gainsboro Rd. PO21: Bog R	.2B 40
Gainsborough Dr. PO20: Sel	.4E 45
Gamecock Ter. PO20: Tang	.1E 19
Garden Av. PO20: Brac	.5G 43
Garden Cl. BN16: Ang	.2F 27
Garden Cott. PO18: Bosh	.4A 14
Garden Ct. PO21: Aldw	.3F 39
Garden Cres. PO22: Barn	.4H 21

Garden Lodge PO21: Pag	.3B 38
(off Pagham Rd.)	
Garland Cl. PO19: Chich	.4E 17
Garland Sq. PO20: Tang	.5E 7
Gaston Av. PO18: Mid L	.1E 5
Gateway Lodge PO22: Felp	.1E 41
(off Felpham Rd.)	
Gaugemaster Ind. Est. BN18: Ford	.4H 23
Gaugemaster Way BN18: Ford	.4H 23
Genoa Cl. BN17: L'ton	.1H 35
George IV Wlk. PO22: Felp	.6F 31
George St. PO19: Chich	.2D 16
Georgian Gdns. BN16: Rust	.1D 36
Gerrard Ho. Bus. Cen. BN16: E Pres	.1E 37
(off Worthing Rd.)	
Gibson Rd. PO20: Tang	.5D 6
Gibson Way PO21: Bog R	.1C 40
Gifford Rd. PO18: Bosh	.2B 14
Gilbert Rd. PO19: Chich	.1B 16
Gilberts, The BN16: Rust	.4H 35
Giles Cl. BN18: Yap	.1C 32
Gill Way PO20: Sel	.3G 45
Gilmore Rd. PO19: Chich	.3F 17
Gilpin Cl. PO19: Fish	.3G 15
Gilwynes PO21: Aldw	.3G 39
Gilwynes Ct. PO21: Aldw	.3G 39
Glade, The PO21: Pag	.5B 38
Gladonian Rd. BN17: Wick	.6E 25
Gladstone Rd. BN18: Yap	.1C 32
Gladstone Ter. BN17: Wick	.6E 25
Glamis Ct. PO21: Bog R	.2C 40
Glamis St. PO21: Bog R	.2C 40
Glebe, The PO20: Tang	.6D 6
Glebe Cl. PO20: Nort	.6A 8
Glenavon M. BN17: Wick	.1D 34
(off Lineside Way)	
Glencathara Rd. PO21: Bog R	.2A 40
Glen Cres. PO20: Sel	.4E 45
Glenelg Cl. PO21: Bers	.5G 29
Glenville Rd. BN16: Rust	.2B 36
Glenway PO22: Bog R	.1C 40
Glenwood Av. PO22: Bog R	.1C 40
Globe Pl. BN17: Wick	.6E 25
Gloster Pl. PO21: Pag	.4C 38
Gloucester La. BN17: L'ton	.2E 35
Gloucester Pl. BN17: L'ton	.2E 35
Gloucester Rd. BN17: L'ton	.2D 34
PO21: Bog R	.2D 40
Gloucester Way PO19: Chich	.6C 4
Glynde Cres. PO22: Felp	.6F 31
Glynn Ho. Cl. PO20: Sel	.4E 45
(off Malthouse Rd.)	
Goathlands Caravan Pk. PO20: Sel	.3C 44
Goda Rd. BN17: L'ton	.2F 35
Godman Cl. PO21: Aldw	.2E 39
Godwin Way PO18: Fish	.1F 15
Goldcrest Av. BN17: Wick	.5D 24
Golden Acre BN16: E Pres	.3G 37
PO21: Pag	.5B 38
Golden Av. BN16: E Pres	.1G 37
Golden Av. Cl. BN16: E Pres	.3G 37
Goldfinch Way PO20: Sel	.2D 44
Golfers La. BN16: Ang	.5C 26
Golf Links La. PO20: Sel	.1D 44
Golf Links Rd. PO22: Felp	.5E 31
(not continuous)	
Goodacres PO22: Barn	.4H 21
Goodhew Cl. BN18: Yap	.6D 22
Goodwood Av. PO22: Felp	.6E 31
Goodwood Cl. BN16: Rust	.1D 36
Goodwood Ct. PO20: Sel	.3E 45
Goodwood Gdns. PO20: Runc	.2A 28
Goodwood Golf Course	.1H 5
Goodwood House	.1A 6
Goodwood Motor Circuit	.4F 5
Goodwood Park Golf Course	.2B 6
Goodwood Pl. PO21: Bog R	.3B 40
(off West St.)	
Gordon Av. PO19: Chich	.6B 16
PO22: Bog R	.1C 40
(not continuous)	
Gordon Av. W. PO22: Bog R	.6C 30
Gordon Ho. PO19: Chich	.3D 16
(off Church Sq.)	
Gordon Ter. BN18: Poling	.1B 26
Gorse Av. BN16: King G	.3H 37
PO22: Felp	.5A 32
Gosden Rd. BN17: L'ton	.1G 35
Gospond Rd. PO22: Barn	.4G 21
Gossamer La. PO21: Aldw	.2E 39
Graffham Cl. PO19: Chich	.4D 4
Grafton Av. PO22: Felp	.5H 31
Grafton Cl. BN16: Rust	.1B 36
Grafton Ct. PO20: Sel	.5E 45
Grafton Rd. PO20: Sel	.6E 45
Graham Rd. BN18: Yap	.2C 32
Granary La. PO20: Sel	.3D 44
Granary Way BN17: Wick	.5E 25
Grand Av. BN17: Wick	.6D 24
Grange Ct. PO21: Aldw	.4F 39
Grange Fld. Way PO21: Aldw	.3E 39
Grange La. PO20: Sel	.1F 45
Grangeway, The BN16: Rust	.2B 36

Grangewood Dr. PO21: Aldw 3E 39
Grant Cl. PO20: Sel 4D 44
Granville Rd. BN17: L'ton 3F 35
Grassmere Cl. BN17: L'ton 6H 25
   PO22: Felp 1E 41
Gratwicke Ct. BN17: Wick 5G 25
                   (off Gratwicke Dr.)
Gratwicke Dr. BN17: Wick 5G 25
Gravel La. PO19: Chich 4F 17
Gravits La. PO21: Bog R 6H 29
Graydon Av. PO19: Chich 5B 16
Graylingwell Cotts. PO19: Chich 5D 4
Graylingwell Dr. PO19: Chich 6E 5
                   (not continuous)
Grayshott Dr. PO22: Bers 5C 30
Grayswood Av. PO20: Brac 5G 43
Green, The PO19: Chich 1F 17
   PO21: Pag 5B 38
Greenacres Ring BN16: Ang 3F 27
Green Bank PO22: Barn 4H 21
Greenbushes Cl. BN16: Rust 3A 36
Green Cl. BN17: L'ton 3E 35
   PO20: E Witt 4E 43
               (off Cakeham Rd.)
Greencourt Dr. PO21: Bers 6H 29
Greenfields BN17: Wick 6C 24
   PO22: Midd S 6B 32
Green La. PO18: Bosh 3B 14
   PO19: Chich 2E 17
   PO20: Oving 6A 18
   PO20: Runc 1A 28
   PO20: Sel 5D 44
Green La. Cl. BN18: Arun 5A 12
Green Lawns Caravan Pk. PO20: Sel 2E 45
Greenlea Av. PO21: Aldw, Pag 3C 38
Green Way PO22: Midd S 6C 32
Greenways PO21: Pag 4C 38
Greenway Wlk. PO20: E Witt 5G 43
Greenwood Av. PO22: Bers, Bog R 5A 30
Greenwood Cl. PO22: Bers 5A 30
Greenwood Dr. BN16: Ang 5E 27
Grenville Gdns. PO19: Chich 5C 16
Grevatt's La. BN17: Climp 4C 32
   BN18: Bils 4C 32
Grevatt's La. W. BN18: Bils 3C 32
Greyfriars Cl. PO21: Aldw 2G 39
Greynville Cl. PO21: Aldw 3D 38
Greystone Av. PO21: Bers 4G 29
Gribble La. PO20: Oving 2C 18
Griffin Cres. BN17: Wick 5E 25
Grooms Cl. BN16: Ang 4F 27
Grosvenor Gdns. PO21: Aldw 2D 38
Grosvenor Rd. PO19: Chich 5C 16
Grosvenor Way PO21: Aldw 2D 38
Grove, The PO22: Felp 1F 41
Grove Cres. BN17: L'ton 1F 35
Grove Pk. PO19: Chich 3A 16
Grove Rd. PO19: Chich 4E 17
   PO20: Sel 5E 45
Guernsey Farm La. PO22: Felp 6H 31
Guilden Rd. PO19: Chich 3E 17
Guildford Pl. PO19: Chich 6C 4
Guildford Rd. BN16: Rust 1D 36
Guildhall
   Chichester 2D 16
Guildhall St. PO19: Chich 2D 16
Gullivers Mead PO22: Felp 4G 31
Gunwin Ct. PO21: Aldw 3E 39

H

Hacketts Rew PO19: Chich 3D 4
Hadlands PO21: Pag 4B 38
Hadley Cl. PO22: Midd S 5B 32
Hailsham Cl. BN16: E Pres 6G 27
Hale Cl. PO20: E Witt 5G 43
Hales Footpath PO22: Felp 6F 31
Haleybridge Wlk. PO20: Tang 6D 6
Halfrey Cl. PO18: Fish 2F 15
Halfrey Rd. PO18: Fish 2F 15
Halliford Dr. PO22: Barn 3H 21
Halliwick Gdns. PO22: Felp 1G 41
HALNAKER 2E 7
Halnaker Barn La. PO18: Box 3A 8
Halnaker Gdns. PO21: Aldw 3D 38
Halson Cl. PO21: Bog R 1B 40
HAM 1B 44
Hambledon Pl. PO21: Bog R 2A 40
Hamble Ter. BN17: Wick 1D 34
Hamilton Cl. BN16: Rust 5A 26
Hamilton Dr. BN16: Rust 5A 26
Hamilton Gdns. PO18: Bosh 2B 14
   PO21: Aldw 3E 39
Ham La. PO20: Tang, Oving 1E 19
Hamlet, The BN17: Climp 2G 33
   PO22: Bog R 5B 30
Ham Mnr. Cl. BN16: Ang 5D 26
Ham Manor Golf Course 5C 26
Ham Mnr. Way BN16: Ang 5D 26
HAMMERPOT 1E 27
Hammond Cl. BN16: Ang 5F 27
Hampden Cl. PO22: Midd S 6C 32

Hampden Pl. PO20: Tang 5E 7
Hampshire Av. PO21: Bog R 6A 30
Hampton Ct. PO21: Bog R 1G 39
Hampton Flds. BN17: Wick 1E 35
Hampton Pl. BN17: Wick 6D 24
Ham Rd. PO20: Sidle 1A 44
HANGLETON 5H 27
Hannah Sq. PO19: Chich 2A 16
Hanover Cl. PO20: Sel 4F 45
Harberton Cres. PO19: Chich 4C 4
Harbour Ct. PO18: Bosh 4B 14
Harbour Park 4E 35
Harbour Rd. PO18: Bosh 5A 14
   PO21: Pag 6A 38
Harbour Vw. Pk. BN17: L'ton 3D 34
Harbour Vw. Rd. PO21: Pag 4A 38
Harbour Way PO18: Bosh 5B 14
Harcourt Way PO20: Sel 3F 45
Hard, The PO22: Midd S 6F 33
Hardham Cl. BN16: Rust 3A 36
Hardham Rd. PO19: Chich 4E 17
Harding Cl. PO20: Sel 2F 45
Hardy Cl. PO22: Felp 6A 32
Harebell Cl. BN17: L'ton 6A 26
Harefield Gdns. PO22: Midd S 6C 32
Harefield Rd. PO22: Midd S 6C 32
Hare La. PO20: Sel 3B 44
Haresfield Ter. PO20: Tang 6E 7
Harfield Ct. PO21: Bog R 2C 40
Harmony Dr. PO20: Brac 6G 43
Harold Cl. PO21: Bers 5G 29
Harrow Dr. PO20: W Witt 4E 43
Harsfold Cl. BN16: Rust 3A 36
Harsfold Rd. BN16: Rust 4A 36
Harting Rd. BN17: Wick 6E 25
Hartings, The PO22: Felp 5A 32
Hartnetts Cotts. BN16: Rust 2A 36
                  (off Sea La.)
Harvester Cl. PO19: Chich 2E 17
Harwood Ind. Est. BN17: L'ton 1D 34
Harwood Rd. BN17: L'ton 1D 34
Harwood Rd. Ent. Units BN17: Wick 1D 34
              (off Harwood Rd.)
Hastings Cl. PO21: Bog R 1G 39
Hatherleigh Cl. PO21: Bog R 6H 29
Hatherleigh Gdns. PO21: Bog R 6H 29
Havelock Cl. PO22: Felp 2E 41
Havelock Rd. PO21: Bog R 1B 40
Haven, The BN17: L'ton 2H 35
Havenstoke Cl. PO19: Chich 6D 4
Havenwood Pk. BN18: Bins 4E 11
Hawke Cl. BN16: Rust 2D 36
Hawker Cl. PO20: Tang 5E 7
Hawkins Cl. PO21: Aldw 3C 38
Hawks Pl. PO22: Bers 5A 30
Hawley Rd. PO22: Felp 3A 36
Hawthorn Cl. BN16: Rust 3B 36
   PO19: Chich 2C 16
Hawthorn Rd. BN17: Wick 5D 24
   PO21: Bog R 2H 39
Hawthorns, The PO21: Bog R 1B 40
Haydon Cl. PO21: Aldw 4D 38
Hayes Cl. PO18: Mid L 1E 5
Hayley's Gdns. PO22: Felp 1F 41
Hay Rd. PO19: Chich 5E 17
Hayter Gdns. PO20: Oving 2D 18
Haywards Cl. PO22: Felp 6F 31
Haywards Pl. PO20: Brac 6H 43
Hazel Gro. BN18: Arun 5H 11
   PO21: Aldw 2E 39
Hazel Lodge BN16: Rust 3B 36
            (off Cudlow Gdn.)
Hazelmead Dr. BN16: E Pres 2F 37
Hazel Rd. BN16: Ang 5F 27
   PO22: Bers 5A 30
Headley Dr. PO22: Bers 5C 30
Hearn Cl. PO22: Felp 6D 6
Hearnfield Rd. BN17: Wick 5E 25
Heathcourt BN17: L'ton 2D 34
Heather Cl. PO19: Chich 4C 16
Heathers, The BN16: Ang 3E 27
Heathfield Av. BN16: Ang 6E 27
Heath Pl. PO22: Bers 4C 30
Hechle Wood PO21: Aldw 3G 39
Hedge End PO22: Barn 3H 21
Hedgerow Cl. PO22: Felp 5G 31
Hedgers Hill BN18: Bins, Walb 6C 10
Hedgeway PO22: Felp 6A 32
Heghbrok Way PO21: Aldw 3H 39
Helyer's Grn. BN17: Wick 1D 34
Hendon Av. BN16: Rust 4H 35
Henfield Way PO22: Felp 5A 32
Henry Av. BN16: Rust 2H 35
Henry Cl. PO19: Chich 3G 17
Henry Fletcher Cl. BN16: Ang 4F 27
Henry St. PO21: Bog R 1C 40
Henty Dr. BN18: Walb 1B 22
Henty Gdns. PO19: Chich 3B 16
Heo Grn. BN17: Wick 6C 24
Herald Dr. PO19: Chich 4D 16
Hercules Pl. PO22: Felp 6A 32
Hereford Cl. PO19: Chich 6C 4
Herington Rd. BN18: Arun 5A 12

Heritage, The PO19: Chich 3E
Heritage Pl. BN16: Rust 3B
             (off Broadmark L
Herne Ct. BN16: Rust 1C
              (off Station F
Herne Gdns. BN16: Rust 1C
Herne La. BN16: Rust 1C
Heron Cl. PO18: Mid L 1C
   PO20: Sel 3B
   PO22: Bers 4A
Heron Ct. PO19: Chich 2G
Herondean PO19: Chich 5C
Heron Mead PO21: Pag 6A
Herons, The PO20: Sel 4D
Heron's Ct. Cl. BN16: Rust 3B
Hersee Way PO20: Sel 4C
Hertford Cl. PO21: Aldw 2G
Heston Gro. PO21: Aldw 4D
Hewarts La. PO21: Aldw 2E
Hide Cl. BN17: Wick 1A
Hide Gdns. BN16: Rust 1A
Highcroft Av. PO22: Bog R 6D
Highcroft Cl. PO22: Bog R 6D
Highcroft Cres. PO22: Bog R 6D
Highdown Cl. BN16: Ang 4F
Highdown Dr. BN17: L'ton, Wick 6C
Highfield BN17: Wick 6C
Highfield Cl. BN16: Ang 4F
Highfield Gdns. BN16: Rust 2A
   PO22: Bog R 6C
Highfield La. PO20: Oving 2D
Highfield Rd. PO22: Bog R 6C
            (not continuou
Highgate Dr. PO21: Bers 5G
Highground La. PO22: Barn 5F
Highland Av. PO19: Chich 1A
Highland Rd. PO19: Chich 5C
High Ridge Cl. BN18: Arun 6A
High St. BN16: Ang 4E
   BN17: L'ton 2E
   BN18: Arun 4C
   PO18: Bosh 5A
   PO19: Chich 1C
   PO20: Oving 3D
   PO20: Sel 4D
   PO21: Bog R 2C
High Trees PO21: Aldw 3G
Highview Rd. PO20: E'gate 2E
Hilary Rd. PO19: Chich 2B
Hillfield Rd. PO20: Sel 6D
Hill La. PO22: Barn 5G
Hill Rd. BN17: L'ton 1F
Hillsboro Rd. PO21: Bog R 1B
Hills Cl. PO21: Bog R 2C
            (off London Rc
Hillside Cres. BN16: Ang 5A
Hill Ter. BN18: Arun 5A
Hillview Cres. BN16: E Pres 1F
Hilton Pk. PO20: E Witt 3F
Hinde Rd. PO22: Felp 6H
Hislop Wlk. PO21: Bog R 2C
HMP Ford BN18: Ford 1G
Hobbs Way BN16: Rust 2B
Hoe La. BN18: Bins 2F
   PO22: Flan 3F
Holdens, The PO18: Bosh 4A
Holdens Farm Caravan Pk. PO20: Brac ..4G
Holford Grn. PO20: Sel 3F
Holland Cl. PO21: Bers 6G
Hollies, The PO21: Bers 6G
Hollist Chase BN17: Wick 5F
Hollist Ct. BN17: Wick 5F
Holly Cl. PO22: Bers 5B
Holly Dr. BN17: Wick 5F
Hollyhock Way BN17: L'ton 6H
Holmdale PO20: E'gate 6E
Holmes Foundation BN18: Arun 5C
            (off Fitzalan Rd
Holmes La. BN16: Rust 3A
Holmes Way BN17: Wick 5F
Holmwood Cl. PO20: W Witt 2B
Homecroft Ho. PO21: Bog R 2A
Homefield Av. PO22: Felp 5H
Homefield Cl. BN16: Rust 1B
Homefield Cres. BN18: Walb 6A
Homelands Av. BN16: E Pres 3F
Homestead, The BN16: E Pres 2F
Homing Gdns. PO22: Bers 4A
Honey La. BN16: Ang 4F
Honeysuckle Cl. BN17: L'ton 6H
Honeysuckle Dr. PO21: Pag 3A
Honeysuckle La. PO20: Sel 3C
Hooe, The BN17: L'ton 2H
Hooe Farm Ind. Est. BN18: Walb 1B
Hook La. PO18: Bosh 6D
   PO20: Ald 2A
   PO21: Pag 3B
   PO21: Pag 1C
Hook La. Cl. PO21: Aldw 2C
Hopgarton, The PO21: Aldw 2F
Hornbeam Cl. PO21: Aldw 3G
Hornet, The PO19: Chich 3E
Horns La. PO21: Pag 4A

Horsefield Rd. PO20: Sel 4D 44
HORSEMERE GREEN 2G 33
Horsemere Grn. La. BN17: Climp ..2F 33
Horse Shoe, The PO20: Sel 4D 44
Horsham Rd. BN17: L'ton ..2G 35
Horsham Rd. W. BN17: L'ton ..1G 35
Horton Pl. BN16: Ang ..5F 27
Hotham Gdns. PO22: Bog R ..1D 40
Hotham Park ..1C 40
Hotham Way PO21: Bog R ..6C 30
  PO22: Bog R ..6C 30
Howard Av. PO20: W Witt ..4C 42
Howard Ho. PO21: Pag ..1H 39
Howard Pl. BN17: L'ton ..2E 35
Howard Rd. BN17: L'ton ..2D 34
  BN18: Arun ..5A 12
Howards Way BN16: Rust ..4A 36
Huddlestones BN16: Ang ..3E 27
Hughes Cl. PO21: Aldw ..1G 39
Humber Cl. BN17: L'ton ..3G 35
Hundredsteddle La. PO20: Bir ..1H 43
Hunnisett Cl. PO20: Sel ..2F 45
Hunston Rd. PO20: Huns, N Mun ..6E 17
Hunters Cl. PO21: Aldw ..4D 38
Hunters Ga. PO20: Tang ..6D 6
Hunters M. BN18: Font, Walb ..5F 9
Hunters Race PO19: Mid L, W Bro ..5A 4
Hunters Way PO19: Chich ..4C 4
Hurst Rd. BN16: E Pres ..1D 36
Hutchinson Cl. BN16: Rust ..6A 26

I

Icarus Way PO22: Felp ..6H 31
Ice House, The ..1C 40
Ilex Cl. BN16: Rust ..3B 36
Ilex Way PO22: Midd S ..5B 32
Infirmary Ter. PO19: Chich ..1C 16
Inglewood Cl. PO21: Aldw ..4D 38
Inglewood Dr. PO21: Aldw ..4C 38
Ingram Cl. BN16: Rust ..2A 36
Innerwyke Cl. PO22: Felp ..6G 31
Iris Cl. BN17: L'ton ..6A 26
Irvine Rd. BN17: L'ton ..3E 35
Island La. PO20: Sel ..3B 44
Island Loop PO20: Sel ..3B 44
Ivanhoe Pl. PO22: Felp ..6H 31
Ivy Cl. PO20: Westg ..2C 20
Ivy Cres. PO22: Bog R ..6C 30
Ivydale Rd. PO21: Bog R ..1H 39
Ivy La. PO20: Westg ..2C 20
  PO22: Bog R ..6C 30
Ivyvine Way PO20: N Mun ..5F 17

J

Jacken Cl. PO22: Felp ..1H 41
James St. PO20: Sel ..5E 45
Jarvis Rd. BN18: Arun ..5A 12
Jasmine Cl. BN17: L'ton ..6H 25
Jaybelle Grange Lodge Pk. BN17: Climp ..3F 33
Jays, The BN17: L'ton ..1E 35
Jays Cl. BN17: L'ton ..1E 35
Jay Wlk. PO19: Chich ..3D 16
  (off St Martins St.)
Jeffreys Av. PO19: Chich ..6D 4
Jerrard Rd. PO20: Tang ..5E 7
Jervis Av. BN16: Rust ..3C 36
Jetty, The PO22: Midd S ..6D 32
Jib Cl. BN17: L'ton ..6H 25
John Arundel Rd. PO19: Chich ..2B 16
Johnson Way BN18: Ford ..1E 33
John St. PO21: Bog R ..2C 40
Jolliffe Rd. PO20: W Witt ..4C 42
Jones Sq. PO20: Sel ..5E 45
Joys Cl. BN17: Wick ..6D 24
Joys Cft. PO19: Chich ..2E 17
Joys Cft. Ct. PO19: Chich ..2E 17
  (off Joys Cft.)
Jubilee Av. BN16: Rust ..1B 36
Jubilee Gdns. PO21: Pag ..4C 38
Jubilee Pde. PO22: Midd S ..6D 32
Jubilee Pl. PO22: Bog R ..6B 30
Jubilee Rd. PO19: Chich ..2D 16
Jubilee Ter. PO19: Chich ..2D 16
June Cl. PO21: Bog R ..5A 38
Juniper Cl. PO22: Midd S ..5B 32
Juxon Cl. PO19: Chich ..4D 16

K

Kandy Pk. BN17: L'ton ..2D 34
Kathleen Gdns. PO19: Chich ..3F 17
Keats Wlk. PO21: Bog R ..2A 40
Keats Way PO19: Chich ..3D 16
Keble Cl. PO21: Aldw ..2G 39
Keelson Way BN17: L'ton ..1H 35
Keepers Wood PO19: Chich ..4C 4

Kelmscott Way PO21: Bers 4H 29
Kendal Cl. BN17: L'ton ..6H 25
Kenhurst BN16: E Pres ..2F 37
Kenilworth Rd. PO21: Bog R ..1H 39
Kenlegh PO21: Aldw ..3G 39
Kensington Rd. PO19: Chich ..3F 17
Kent Rd. BN17: L'ton ..1E 35
  PO19: Chich ..2E 17
Kerry Gdns. BN16: E Pres ..1F 37
Kestrel Cl. PO20: E Witt ..5F 43
Kestrel Ct. PO19: Chich ..2G 17
  PO21: Pag ..6A 38
Kestrel Way BN17: Wick ..5D 24
Ketch Rd. BN17: L'ton ..4F 35
Kew Gdns. PO21: Bog R ..1G 39
Kidd Rd. PO19: Chich ..6E 5
Kiln Wlk. PO18: Westh ..6H 5
Kilnwood Cl. PO20: Sel ..4F 45
Kilwich Cl. PO22: Midd S ..5A 32
Kimberry BN17: Wick ..6D 24
Kimbridge Pk. PO20: E Witt ..5F 43
  (off Nagels Cl.)
Kimbridge Rd. PO20: E Witt ..5F 43
Kingfisher Ct. PO22: Midd S ..6C 32
Kingfisher Dr. BN17: Wick ..5D 24
Kingfisher Pde. PO20: E Witt ..4E 43
  (off Cakeham Rd.)
King George Ct. PO21: Bog R ..1A 40
King George Gdns. PO19: Chich ..1C 16
Kingley Va. PO20: Sel ..2E 45
Kingmere BN17: L'ton ..3F 35
  (off South Ter.)
Kings Arms Hill BN18: Arun ..4C 12
Kings Av. PO19: Chich ..5C 16
Kings Cl. BN18: Yap ..6C 22
Kings Ct. PO20: Sel ..3E 45
  PO21: Bog R ..2D 40
  (off The Esplanade)
King's Dr. PO21: Pag ..5C 38
KINGSHAM ..5D 16
Kingsham Av. PO19: Chich ..4E 17
Kingsham Rd. PO19: Chich ..4D 16
Kingsmead BN17: Wick ..4D 24
  PO22: Felp ..1E 41
Kingsmead Gdns. PO22: Midd S ..5C 32
Kingsmead Rd. PO22: Midd S ..5D 32
Kingsmill Rd. PO22: Barn ..3H 21
King's Pde. PO21: Aldw ..3H 39
KINGSTON GORSE ..3H 37
Kingston La.
  BN16: E Pres, King G ..1G 37
King St. BN18: Arun ..4B 12
Kingsway PO20: Sel ..4E 39
  PO21: Aldw ..4E 39
Kinleside Way BN16: Ang ..5F 27
Kirdford Cl. BN16: Rust ..3A 36
Kirdford Rd. BN18: Arun ..5B 12
Kirkby Cl. PO18: Box ..4E 7
Kirkland Cl. BN16: Rust ..2A 36
Kithurst Cl. BN16: E Pres ..3D 36
Knap La. PO20: Sel ..4D 44
Knightscroft Av. BN16: Rust ..3B 36
Knightscroft Cl. BN16: Rust ..3A 36
Kynon Gdns. PO22: Midd S ..5A 32
Kyoto Ct. PO21: Bog R ..2H 39

L

Laburnum Gro. PO19: Chich ..4D 16
  PO22: Bers, Bog R ..5B 30
Laburnum M. PO21: Bog R ..2C 40
  (off Lyon St.)
Laburnum Wlk. BN16: Rust ..1A 36
Lacey Ho. PO19: Chich ..4C 16
Lacock Cl. PO20: Brac ..6H 43
Ladbrooke Cl. BN16: Rust ..5E 27
LAGNESS ..5B 28
Lagness Rd. PO20: N Mun, Runc ..2A 28
Lagoon Rd. PO21: Pag ..6A 38
Lakeland Av. PO21: Pag ..3H 29
Lakelands Dr. PO20: N Mun ..5F 17
Lake La. PO22: Barn, Yap ..3H 21
Lake Rd. PO19: Chich ..3F 17
Lakeside Holiday Village PO20: N Mun ..6G 17
Lakeside Superbowl
  Chichester ..4C 16
Lake Vw. PO21: Pag ..4B 38
Lammas Cl. BN17: Wick ..6F 25
Lamorna Gdns. PO20: Westg ..3C 20
Lancaster Pl. PO21: Pag ..5B 30
Lancastrian Grange PO19: Chich ..2C 16
Landrery Ind. Estate, The PO20: Sel ..3D 44
Landseer Dr. PO20: Sel ..4F 45
Lane, The PO19: Chich ..5D 4
Lane End Farm Caravan Site
  PO22: Midd S ..5D 32
Lane End Rd. PO22: Midd S ..6D 32
Langdale Av. PO19: Chich ..5E 17
Langley Gro. PO21: Aldw ..4D 38
Langmead Cl. BN17: Climp ..3H 33
Langton Cl. PO20: Sel ..5D 44
Langton Rd. PO19: Chich ..2B 16

Lansdowne Cl. BN16: Ang 3E 27
  (Huddlestones)
  BN16: Ang 5F 27
  (Willowood Cl.)
Lansdowne Rd. BN16: Ang ..4E 27
  BN17: Wick ..6E 25
Lansdowne Way BN16: Ang ..3E 27
Lanyards BN17: L'ton ..6H 25
Lapwing Ct. PO20: Sel ..3D 44
Larch Cl. BN16: Rust ..2C 36
  PO19: Chich ..5C 4
  PO22: Bers ..4B 30
Larchfield Cl. PO21: Aldw ..4E 39
Large Acres PO20: Sel ..4D 44
Larkspur Cl. BN17: L'ton ..6H 25
Lashmar Rd. BN16: E Pres ..1F 37
Latham Cl. BN17: Wick ..1C 34
Latham Rd. PO20: Sel ..5D 44
Laurel Dr. PO21: Pag ..3A 38
Laurel Gro. PO22: Bers ..5B 30
Lauren Gdns. PO22: Felp ..6G 31
Lavant Down Rd. PO18: Mid L ..1E 5
Lavant Rd. PO18: Mid L ..2C 4
  PO19: Mid L, Chich ..2C 4
Lavender Cl. PO22: Midd S ..5B 32
Lavinia Ct. PO21: Bog R ..1G 39
Lavinia Way BN16: E Pres ..2F 37
Lawn, The PO21: Aldw ..3F 39
Lawrence Av. BN16: Rust ..1C 36
Lawrence Cl. PO20: Sel ..5E 45
Layne, The PO22: Midd S ..6D 32
Leaholme PO19: Chich ..3F 17
Leaman Cl. PO22: Midd S ..6C 32
Leander Rd. PO18: Bosh ..4B 14
Leas, The BN16: Rust ..6D 26
Leas Ct. PO22: Bog R ..6B 30
Leatherbottle La. PO19: Chich ..3F 17
Ledbury Way PO21: Pag ..3C 38
Ledra Dr. PO21: Pag ..5C 38
Leecroft PO21: Aldw ..3F 39
Leeward Rd. BN17: L'ton ..2H 35
Legion Way PO20: E Witt ..5F 43
Leigh Rd. PO19: Chich ..4C 16
Leinster Gdns. PO22: Felp ..6A 32
Lennox Rd. PO19: Chich ..2E 17
Lennox St. PO21: Bog R ..3C 40
Leonora Dr. PO21: Aldw, Pag ..3C 38
Leopold Ct. PO22: Felp ..6F 31
Level Mare La. PO20: E'gate, Font ..4C 8
Leverton Av. PO22: Felp ..6A 32
Lewes Cl. PO21: Bog R ..1G 39
Lewis La. BN18: Ford ..1E 33
Lewis Rd. PO19: Chich ..2E 17
  PO20: Sel ..4D 44
Ley Rd. PO22: Felp ..6G 31
Lichfield Gdns. PO21: Aldw ..2F 39
LIDSEY ..6C 20
Lidsey Caravan Pk. PO22: Shrip ..1C 30
Lidsey La. PO21: Bers ..4G 29
Lidsey Rd. PO20: W'gate ..4C 20
  PO22: Shrip, W'gate ..1C 30
Lifeboat Museum, The
  Selsey ..5F 45
Lifeboat Station
  Littlehampton 3E 35
  (off Surrey St.)
Lifeboat Way PO20: Sel ..6E 45
Lilac Cl. BN17: L'ton ..6H 25
  PO22: Midd S ..5B 32
Lillian Ter. BN18: Poling ..1B 26
Lillywhite Rd. PO18: Westh ..6H 5
Lime Av. PO20: Westg ..2D 20
Lime Cl. PO19: Chich ..2E 17
Lime Gro. BN16: Ang ..5E 27
Lime Kiln Coppice PO22: Felp ..5F 31
Limes, The BN16: Rust ..1B 36
  BN18: Yap ..6C 22
Limetree Cl. BN16: E Pres ..1E 37
Limmard Way PO22: Felp ..1H 41
Limmer La. PO22: Felp ..1F 41
Lincoln Av. PO21: Aldw ..1D 38
Lincoln Grn. PO19: Chich ..6C 4
Linden Pk. BN17: L'ton ..2D 34
Linden Rd. BN17: L'ton ..2D 34
  PO21: Bog R ..1A 40
Lindsey Ct. PO22: Felp ..5F 31
Lineside Ind. Est. BN17: Wick ..1C 34
Lineside Way BN17: Wick ..1C 34
Linfield Cl. BN16: Ang ..5F 27
Lingfield Way PO20: Sel ..4E 45
Links, The PO20: Sel ..2E 45
Links Av. PO22: Felp ..1E 41
Link Way PO21: Pag ..4B 38
Linnet Cl. BN17: Wick ..5D 24
Lion Ct. PO21: Pag ..3C 38
  (off Mill Pk. Rd.)
Lionel Av. PO22: Felp ..5H 31
Lion Rd. PO21: Pag ..3B 38
Lion St. PO19: Chich ..3D 16
Litten Ter. PO19: Chich ..2D 16
Little Babbsham PO21: Aldw ..3F 39
Little Breach PO19: Chich ..6C 4
Littlefield Cl. PO20: Sel ..4E 45

Littlefield Rd. PO19: Chich 4E 17
LITTLEHAMPTON .2E 35
Littlehampton By-Pass BN17: L'ton, Wick 6C 24
Littlehampton Caravan Club Site BN17: Wick . . .4E 35
Littlehampton Golf Course 1E 35
Littlehampton Marina BN17: L'ton 2C 34
Littlehampton Mus. 2F 35
Littlehampton Rd. BN12: Fer 6H 27
BN16: Fer 6H 27
Littlehampton Station (Rail) 2E 35
Littlehampton Swimming & Sports Cen. 4G 35
LITTLE HEATH 2E 9
Littleheath Rd. BN18: Font 4D 8
Little High St. PO21: Bog R 3B 40
Little London PO19: Chich 3D 16
Lizard Head BN17: L'ton 1H 35
Lloyd Goring Cl. BN16: Ang 3E 27
Lloyd Rd. PO19: Chich 6D 4
Loats La. PO21: Bers 4G 29
Lobster La. PO20: Sel 3B 44
Locksash Cl. PO20: W Witt 1A 42
Lodge Cl. PO22: Midd S 6D 32
Lodge Ct. PO21: Aldw 3F 39
Lodsworth PO21: Pag 2C 38
London Rd. BN18: Arun 1H 11
BN18: Font 4F 9
PO21: Bog R 2C 40
Long Acre PO20: Sel 5D 44
Longacre La. PO20: Sel 5D 44
Longacre Pk. BN18: Yap 4C 22
Longbrook PO22: Felp 2E 41
Longford Rd. PO21: Bog R 2B 40
Longlands Rd. PO20: E Witt 5D 42
Long La. BN18: Arun 2F 11
Long Mead BN18: Walb 6A 10
Longport PO22: Felp 1G 41
Longships BN17: L'ton 1H 35
Look & Sea! 3E 35
Loop, The PO22: Felp 1H 41
Loudoun Rd. BN17: L'ton 1D 34
Lovells Cl. PO21: Aldw 3C 38
Loveys Rd. BN18: Yap 1C 32
Lwr. Bognor Rd. PO20: Lag 5C 28
PO21: Aldw, Lag 5C 28
Lower Rd. PO18: E Lav 2D 4
Lwr. Walls Wlk. PO19: Chich 3D 16
(off Keats Way)
Loxwood BN16: E Pres 6G 27
Lucerne Ct. PO21: Aldw 3F 39
Lucking La. PO22: Midd S 6C 32
Lucksfield Way BN16: Ang 4F 27
Ludlow Cl. PO21: Aldw 3F 39
Lundy Cl. BN17: L'ton 3H 35
Lupin Cl. BN17: L'ton 6H 25
Lychgates, The BN18: Yap 5C 22
LYMINSTER 3E 25
Lyminster Rd. BN17: Lym, Wick 3E 25
BN18: Cross 6E 13
Lyndhurst Rd. PO19: Chich 4E 17
Lyon St. PO21: Bog R 2C 40
Lyon St. W. PO21: Bog R 2C 40
Lysander Way PO20: Tang 6E 7

M

Mackeral Cl. PO20: Sel 3B 44
Mackintosh Dr. PO21: Bers 4H 29
Macklin Rd. PO22: Bog R 1D 40
McNair Ct. PO20: Sel 3D 44
McRae Ct. PO20: Sel 4D 44
Madehurst Cl. BN16: E Pres 3D 36
Madehurst Cl. BN17: L'ton 2E 35
(off Gloucester Rd.)
Madehurst Cl. BN18: Made 1D 10
Madehurst Way BN17: L'ton 1E 35
Madeira Av. PO22: Bog R 1D 40
Madeira Pde. PO22: Bog R 6D 30
Madgwick La. PO18: Westh 6G 5
PO19: Westh 6G 5
Magistrates' Court
Chichester 4D 16
Magpie La. PO20: Sel 2B 44
Main Dr. PO22: Midd S 6C 32
Mainland Av. PO20: N Mun 6F 17
Main Rd. BN18: Yap 6C 22
PO18: Bosh, Fish 2A 14
Malcolm Rd. PO20: Tang 5D 6
(not continuous)
Malden Way PO20: Sel 4D 44
Malin Rd. BN17: L'ton 2H 35
Mallard Cres. PO21: Pag 6A 38
Mallards La. PO20: Sel 3B 44
Mallon Dene BN16: Rust 3B 36
Malmayne Ct. PO21: Aldw 2F 39
Malthouse Cl. BN18: Arun 5B 12
Malthouse Cotts. PO20: W Witt 1C 42
Malthouse Pas. BN17: Wick 1E 35
Malthouse Rd. PO20: Sel 4E 45
Maltings, The PO19: Chich 3C 16
Maltravers Dr. BN17: L'ton 3F 35
Maltravers Rd. BN17: L'ton 3F 35
Maltravers St. BN18: Arun 5B 12

Malvern Way PO21: Pag 4C 38
Manet Sq. PO22: Bers 5A 30
Manning Rd. BN17: Wick 6D 24
Mannock Rd. PO20: Tang 6C 6
Manor Cl. BN16: E Pres 2E 37
PO19: Chich 6C 16
PO22: Felp 1F 41
Manor Copse PO22: Felp 1F 41
Manor Ct. PO22: Midd S 6E 33
(off Manor Way)
Mnr. Farm Cl. PO20: Sel 3E 45
Mnr. Farm Ct. PO20: Sel 3E 45
PO22: Midd S 6E 33
Manor Gdns. BN16: Rust 2A 36
Manor La. PO20: Sel 3F 45
Manor Pk. PO21: Pag 4B 38
Manor Pl. PO21: Bog R 3B 40
Manor Rd. BN16: E Pres 2E 37
BN16: Rust 1A 36
PO20: Sel 4E 45
Manor Vs. PO18: Bosh 4B 14
Manor Way PO21: Aldw 4C 38
PO22: Midd S 6E 33
Mansergh Rd. PO19: Chich 6E 5
Manser Rd. BN18: Walb 6C 10
Mansfield Rd.
PO22: Bers, Bog R 6A 30
Mant Cl. BN17: Climp 2G 33
Mantling Rd. BN17: L'ton 1E 35
Manton Cl. PO20: Brac 6H 43
Maple Cl. PO22: Midd S 5B 32
Maple Gdns. PO22: Bers 4B 30
Maplehurst Rd. PO19: Chich 4E 5
Maple Pde. BN18: Walb 1B 22
(off Maple Rd.)
Maple Rd. BN18: Walb 1B 22
Maples, The PO21: Bog R 2A 40
(off Hambledon Pl.)
Maple Wlk. BN16: Rust 1B 36
Marama Gdns. BN16: Rust 4A 36
March Cl. PO21: Aldw 2D 38
March Sq. PO19: Chich 4D 4
Marchwell Ind. Est. PO19: Chich 5E 5
Marchwood PO19: Chich 4D 4
Marchwood Ga. PO19: Chich 4D 4
Marchwood M. PO19: Chich 4D 4
Marcuse Flds. PO18: Bosh 3A 14
Marden Av. PO19: Chich 6B 16
Marden Ho. BN17: Wick 6C 24
PO22: Barn 3H 21
Margaret Cl. PO21: Aldw 2F 39
Marian Way PO21: Bog R 2D 40
Marigolds, The PO22: Shrip 2C 30
Marigolds Lodge BN16: Rust 3A 36
(off Holmes La.)
Marine Cl. PO20: W Witt 5D 42
Marine Cl. BN17: L'ton 3F 35
PO21: Aldw 3A 40
(off Nyewood La.)
Marine Dr. PO20: Sel 4F 45
PO20: W Witt 4C 42
Marine Dr. W. PO20: W Witt 4C 42
PO21: Aldw, Bog R 3H 39
Marine Gdns. PO20: Sel 6D 44
Marine Pde. PO21: Bog R 3A 40
Mariners PO21: Aldw 3G 39
Mariners Quay BN17: L'ton 2D 34
Mariners Wlk. BN16: Rust 3C 36
Marineside PO20: Brac 6G 43
Marisfield Pl. PO20: Sel 3F 45
Market Av. PO19: Chich 4D 16
Market Cl. PO22: Barn 3G 21
Market Place
Chichester 3D 16
Market Rd. PO19: Chich 3D 16
Market St. PO21: Bog R 3B 40
Markfield PO22: Bers 3G 29
Marlborough Cl. PO19: Chich 3G 17
Marlborough Ct. PO21: Aldw 6G 29
Marlowe Cl. PO22: Midd S 5B 32
Marlpit La. PO20: Oving 3B 18
Marquis Way PO21: Aldw 4F 39
Marshall Av. PO21: Bog R 1A 40
Marshall Cl. PO22: Barn 4G 21
Marsh Barns PO20: Runc 1A 28
Marsh La. PO18: E Lav 1F 5
PO18: Tang 5H 7
PO20: Oving, Runc 3B 18
PO20: Tang 5G 7
Martlets Ct. BN18: Arun 5C 12
Martlet Way PO21: Pag 6A 38
Marylands Cres. PO22: Bog R 6D 30
Matform Bus. Cen. PO19: Chich 4B 16
MAUDLIN 6A 6
Mauldmare Cl. PO21: Aldw 3G 39
Maxwell Rd. BN17: L'ton 2D 34
BN18: Arun 6A 12

May Cl. BN17: Climp 2G 3
PO22: Bog R 6C 3
Mayfair Ct. PO19: Chich 2C 1
Mayfield BN16: E Pres 6F 27
Mayfield Cl. PO21: Pag 2C 3
Mayfield Rd. PO21: Bog R 1H 3
Mayflower Way BN16: Ang 6F 27
Maynards Caravan & Camping Site
BN18: Cross 6E 1
Maypole La. PO21: Yap 4C 2
Maypole La. Caravan Site BN18: Yap 4C 2
Mayridge PO20: Sel .3B 4
Maytree Cl. BN16: Ang 5E 2
Maytree Way PO20: N Nun 5G 1
Mead Cl. PO22: Bog R 1C 4
Meaden Way PO22: Felp 5G 3
Mead La. PO21: Bog R 1C 4
PO22: Bog R 1C 4
Meadow Cl. PO18: Mid L 2C 4
Meadow Ct. PO22: Midd S 5A 32
Meadowfield Dr. PO19: Chich 2E 1
Meadowland PO20: Sel 5D 44
Meadow La. PO20: W Witt 1B 42
Meadow Pk. BN16: E Pres 2G 3
Meadows, The BN18: Walb 1A 22
PO19: Chich 6B 16
Meadowside BN16: Ang 3F 27
Meadowside Wlk. PO20: Tang 5E 7
Meadows Rd. PO20: E Witt 4F 43
Meadow Wlk. PO22: Midd S 6D 32
Meadow Way BN17: L'ton 2G 35
PO20: Tang 6D 6
PO20: Westg 3C 20
PO21: Aldw 5C 38
PO22: Bers 5H 29
Meadsway BN18: Slind 3A 10
Meadway BN16: Rust 2C 36
Medmerry Beach PO20: Sel 3A 44
Medmerry Mill 4B 44
Melanie's Gdns. PO21: Bog R 1C 4
(off Mead La.)
Melbourne Rd. PO19: Chich 2E 1
Mendip Cl. BN16: E Pres 1F 37
Mendip Ct. BN16: Rust 1B 36
Merchant St. PO21: Bog R 2B 40
(off Mead La.)
Mere Cl. PO20: Brac 6G 43
Merlin Way PO22: Midd S 5A 32
Merrion Av. PO22: Bog R 6A 30
Merry End PO22: Midd S 6A 32
Merryfield Cres. BN16: Ang 3F 27
Merryfield Dr. PO20: Sel 4F 45
Merryweather Rd. PO18: Bosh 4A 14
MERSTON 6B 18
Merston Pl. PO21: Bers 4G 29
Merton Av. BN16: Rust 3C 36
Merton Cl. PO21: Aldw 1F 39
Merton Dr. BN17: L'ton 1E 35
Mews, The PO21: Bog R 2B 40
(off Merchant St.)
PO22: Bog R 1D 40
(off Mead La.)
Mewsbrook Park 3H 35
Michel Gro. BN16: E Pres 2D 36
Micklam Cl. PO21: Aldw 3D 38
Midacre Cl. PO22: Felp 5F 31
Middlefield PO20: W Witt 2B 42
Middle Mead BN17: L'ton 2H 35
Middleton Bus. Pk. PO22: Midd S 5C 32
Middleton Cl. PO20: E Witt 5G 43
Middleton Gdns. PO20: Tang 5E 7
MIDDLETON-ON-SEA 6B 32
Middleton Rd. PO22: Felp, Midd S 6H 31
Middle Wlk. BN16: Rust 3E 37
Middle Way BN16: King G 3H 37
Midholme BN16: E Pres 2E 37
Midhurst Rd. PO18: Mid L 1E 5
Mid La. BN18: Slind .3A 10
MID LAVANT 1C 4
Midway, The PO22: Felp 1F 41
Miles Cl. BN18: Ford .1E 33
Miles Cotts. PO18: Bosh 4B 14
Millars Ct. PO21: Pag 4C 38
Mill Cl. BN16: Rust 1C 36
PO19: Fish 3G 15
Millers, The BN18: Yap 1C 32
Millers Cl. BN16: Rust 1C 36
Millfarm Dr. PO21: Pag 3A 38
Millfarm Est. PO21: Pag 3B 38
Millfield Cl. BN16: Rust 4A 36
PO19: Chich 1F 17
Mill Gdns. PO20: E Witt 4E 43
Milliers Cl. BN16: E Pres 1E 37
Millington Dr. PO20: Sel 2E 45
Mill La. BN16: Rust 1C 36
BN17: Wick 4E 25
BN18: Arun 4C 12
BN18: Slind 1H 9
BN18: Walb 6A 10
PO18: Hal 1G 7
PO19: Fish 3G 15
PO20: Sel 4B 44
Mill Pk. Rd. PO21: Pag 3B 38
Mill Pond Way BN16: E Pres 1E 37

Mill Rd. BN16: Ang 4E 27
  BN18: Arun 3C 12
  BN18: Slind 3A 10
Mill Rd. Av. BN16: Ang 4E 27
Mill Vw. Cl. PO21: Pag 3B 38
Mill Vw. Rd. BN18: Yap 1C 32
Millwood Ct. PO19: Chich 2C 16
Milton Av. BN16: Rust 3A 36
Milton Cl. BN16: Rust 2A 36
Milton Pl. PO22: Felp 5G 31
  (off Broom Fld. Way)
Minster Ct. BN17: Wick 5D 24
Minton Rd. PO22: Felp 1F 41
Mitre Cl. PO19: Chich 2B 16
Mixon Cl. PO20: Sel 5E 45
Mole, The BN17: L'ton 2H 35
Mons Av. PO21: Bog R 6A 30
Montagu Pl. PO19: Chich 1B 16
Montalan Cres. PO20: Sel 3B 44
Monterey Gdns. PO21: Bog R 1H 39
Monterey Pines PO22: Felp 1F 41
Montgomeri Dr. BN16: Rust 6A 26
Montgomery Dr. PO22: Midd S 5A 32
Montpelier Rd. BN18: E Pres 2F 37
Moore Pl. PO21: Bog R 1B 40
  (off Victoria Dr.)
Moorhen Way PO22: Bers 5A 30
Moorings, The BN17: L'ton 1H 35
Morants Cl. PO19: Chich 1F 17
Moraunt Dr. PO22: Midd S 5A 32
Moreton Rd. PO18: Bosh 4A 14
Mornington Cres. PO22: Felp 6F 31
Morrells Wlk. PO21: Bers 4G 29
Mosse Gdns. PO19: Fish 2G 15
Mountbatten Ct. BN17: L'ton 1H 35
  (off Ensign Way)
  PO21: Bog R 3C 40
Mount La. PO19: Chich 3C 16
Mt. Pleasant BN18: Arun 4B 12
Mountwood Rd. PO20: Sel 3F 45
M'Tongue Av. PO18: Bosh 2B 14
Mudberry La. PO18: Bosh 1A 14
Mulberry Ct. PO20: Sel 4D 44
  (off East St.)
  PO21: Pag 6B 38
Mulberry Hollow BN16: Ang 5C 26
Mulberry Lodge BN16: Rust 2B 36
  (off Cudlow Gdn.)
Mumford Pl. PO19: Chich 4E 17
Munmere Way BN16: Rust 1D 36
Murina Av. PO21: Bog R 6B 30
Murray Rd. PO20: Sel 5C 44
Murrell Gdns. PO22: Barn 2F 21
Mustang Cl. BN18: Ford 1E 33
Myrtle Copse PO22: Felp 5G 31
Myrtle Gro. BN16: E Pres 2E 37

N

Nab Tower La. PO20: Sel 3A 44
Nab Wlk. PO20: E Witt 5E 43
Nagels Cl. PO20: E Witt 5F 43
Naiad Gdns. PO22: Felp 6A 32
Nash Way BN18: Walb 6A 10
Naunton Rd. PO19: Chich 5D 4
Needlemakers PO22: Chich 3E 17
Nelson Cl. PO20: Tang 5E 7
Nelson Rd. PO21: Bog R 2H 39
Nelson Row BN18: Ford 6H 23
Neptune Ct. PO22: Felp 1H 41
Neptune Way BN17: L'ton, Rust 3H 35
Netherton Cl. PO20: Sel 4E 45
Netley Ct. BN17: L'ton 2E 35
Nettleton Av. PO20: Tang 5D 6
Neville Duke Way PO20: Tang 5E 7
Neville Rd. PO19: Chich 2A 16
  PO22: Bog R 1C 40
New Barn Hill PO18: Box, Good, Hal 2B 6
New Barn La. PO21: Bers 4G 29
  PO22: Felp 5G 31
New Courtwick La. BN17: Wick 5D 24
Newfield Rd. PO20: Sel 3G 45
Newhall Cl. PO21: Bog R 2G 39
Newlands La. PO19: Chich 1B 16
New Pde. PO20: Sel 4D 44
  PO20: W Witt 4D 42
  (off Cakeham Rd.)
New Pk. Rd. PO19: Chich 2D 16
Newport Dr. PO19: Fish 2G 15
New Rd. BN16: Ang, Rust 6C 26
  BN17: L'ton 3E 35
  PO18: E Lav, Good 1E 5
New Ter. BN18: Poling 1B 26
New Town PO19: Chich 3D 16
Newtown Av. PO21: Bers 5H 29
Nicolson Cl. PO20: Tang 5D 6
Nightingale Ct. PO22: Midd S 6C 32
Nightingale Way PO20: Sel 2D 44
Nimbus Cl. BN17: L'ton 1B 26
Nineveh Shipyard BN18: Arun 5C 12
Nook Caravan Park, The PO20: Sel 3C 44
Nookery, The BN16: E Pres 2F 37

Nor'bren Av. PO21: Bers 6H 29
Nordseter Lodge BN16: Rust 3A 36
  (off Sea La.)
Norfolk Cl. PO21: Bog R 3A 40
Norfolk Cotts. BN18: Burp 1H 13
Norfolk Ct. BN16: Rust 3A 36
  (off Chanctonbury Rd.)
Norfolk Gdns. BN17: L'ton 3G 35
Norfolk M. BN17: L'ton 3G 35
  (off Norfolk Pl.)
Norfolk Pl. BN17: L'ton 3G 35
Norfolk Rd. BN17: L'ton 4G 35
Norfolk Sq. PO21: Bog R 3A 40
Norfolk St. PO21: Bog R 3C 40
Norfolk Way PO22: Midd S 6D 32
Norman Cl. PO21: Bog R 2G 35
Normandy Ct. PO19: Chich 2E 17
  (off Joys Cft.)
Normandy Dr. BN16: E Pres 3F 37
Normandy La. BN16: E Pres 3F 37
Normanhurst Cl. BN16: Rust 3B 36
Norman's Dr. PO22: Felp 5G 31
Normanton Av. PO21: Bog R 2A 40
Norman Way PO22: Midd S 6C 32
North Av. PO22: Midd S 6C 32
North Av. E. PO22: Midd S 6C 32
North Av. Sth. PO22: Midd S 6C 32
NORTH BERSTED 5H 29
Nth. Bersted St. PO22: Bers 5H 29
Northcliffe Rd. PO22: Bog R 1D 40
North Cl. PO19: Chich 3D 16
Northcote Rd. PO21: Bog R 1H 39
North Ct. Cl. BN16: Rust 1C 36
North Dr. BN16: Ang 5E 27
NORTH END 4D 22
North End Rd. BN18: Yap 6C 22
Northern Cres. PO20: E Witt 4E 43
North Fld. PO20: W Witt 1B 42
Northfield PO20: Sel 4F 45
Northfields La. PO20: Westg 1C 20
Northgate PO19: Chich 2D 16
  (off Northgate)
North Ham Rd. BN17: L'ton 1E 35
North La. BN16: E Pres 1G 37
  BN16: Rust 1A 36
North Pallant PO19: Chich 3D 16
North Pk. BN17: L'ton 2D 34
North Pl. BN17: L'ton 3F 35
North Pound BN18: Walb 6A 10
North Rd. PO18: Bosh 2B 14
  PO20: Sel 4E 45
  PO22: Felp 5F 31
Northside PO18: Mid L 1E 5
North St. BN17: Wick 6E 25
  PO19: Chich 3D 16
North Walls PO19: Chich 2C 16
North Way PO22: Felp 1E 41
Northway Rd. BN17: Wick 5E 25
Northwyke Cl. PO22: Felp 6H 31
Northwyke Rd. PO22: Felp 6H 31
NORTON 6A 8
Norton La. PO18: Nort 6A 8
  PO20: Nort 6A 8
Norway La. BN17: L'ton 5H 25
  (Rustington By-Pass)
  BN17: L'ton 6G 25
  (The Poplars)
Norwich Rd. PO19: Chich 1C 16
Novium Museum, The 3C 16
Nuffield Cl. PO21: Aldw 2F 39
Nuffield Health Club
  Chichester 4C 16
Nunnington Farm Caravan & Camping Pk.
  PO20: W Witt 1C 42
Nurseries, The PO21: Aldw 2D 38
Nursery Cl. BN16: E Pres 3F 37
  PO22: Barn 3G 21
Nursery Gdns. BN17: Wick 6E 25
  PO19: Chich 4E 17
Nursery La. PO19: Fish 2G 15
Nursery Rd. BN16: Ang 5F 27
NYETIMBER 4B 38
Nyetimber Cl. PO21: Aldw 3C 38
Nyetimber Cres. PO21: Pag 3C 38
Nyetimber La. PO21: Aldw, Pag 3B 38
Nyetimber Mill PO21: Pag 3B 38
Nyetimbers, The PO21: Pag 3B 38
Nyewood Gdns. PO21: Bog R 2A 40
Nyewood Lane 2H 39
Nyewood La. PO21: Aldw, Bog R 1A 40
Nyewood Pl. PO21: Bog R 3A 40
NYTON 1B 20
Nyton Rd. PO18: Tang 5H 7
  PO20: E'gate, Westg 1A 20

O

Oak Av. PO19: Chich 2B 16
Oak Cl. PO19: Chich 2B 16
  PO22: Bers 5B 30
Oakcroft Gdns. BN17: L'ton 6G 25

Oak End BN18: Arun 5H 11
Oakfield Av. PO20: E Witt 4E 43
Oakfield Rd. PO20: E Witt 4E 43
Oakford Pk. PO18: Box 2F 7
Oak Gro. PO22: Bog R 5B 30
Oakhurst Gdns. BN16: Rust 1D 36
Oakland Ct. BN17: L'ton 3F 35
  PO21: Pag 3B 38
  (off Nyetimber La.)
Oaklands Ct. PO19: Chich 1D 16
  (off Somerstown)
Oaklands Park 1D 16
Oaklands Way PO19: Chich 2D 16
  PO20: N Mun 5G 17
Oakley Gdns. BN16: E Pres 2F 37
Oaks, The BN16: Rust 2D 36
  PO21: Aldw 2F 39
Oaks Cl. PO20: N Mun 5G 17
Oaks M. PO21: Aldw 2F 39
Oak Tree Cl. PO21: Pag 3A 38
Oak Tree La. PO20: W'gate 4C 20
Oakwood Cl. PO20: Tang 5E 7
Oakwood Ct. PO21: Bog R 1B 40
  (off Victoria Dr.)
Oakwood Dr. BN16: Ang 5F 27
Oakwood Gdns. PO21: Bog R 1B 40
Ockley Cl. PO21: Bog R 2B 40
Ockley Rd. PO21: Bog R 2B 40
OFFHAM 1E 13
Old Arundel Rd. PO18: Westh 5A 6
Old Bakery Gdns. PO19: Chich 4E 17
Old Bakery M. PO20: Sel 4E 45
Old Barn Cl. PO21: Pag 3B 38
Old Bridge Rd. PO18: Bosh 2A 14
Old Broyle Rd. PO19: W Bro, Chich 5A 4
Old Canal Basin, The BN18: Ford 5H 23
Old Canal Caravan Site PO22: Shrip 6C 20
Old Coastguards PO22: Felp 1E 41
Old Cottage Cl. PO20: Tang 6D 6
Old Dairy La. PO20: Nort 5A 8
Older Way BN16: Ang 3E 27
Old Farm Cl. PO20: Brac 6G 43
  PO21: Aldw 3E 39
Old Farm Dr. PO20: Westg 2C 20
Old Farm Rd. PO20: Sel 3C 44
Old Granary, The PO20: Box 3E 7
Oldlands Way PO22: Bers 4D 30
Old Manor Ho. Gdns. PO22: Felp 6G 31
Old Manor Rd. BN16: Rust 1A 36
Old Market Av. PO20: Tang 3D 16
Old Mead Rd. BN17: Wick 4D 24
Old Mill, The BN18: Arun 4C 12
  (off River Rd.)
Old Mill La. BN16: Ang 4F 27
Old Moat Cl. PO22: Shrip 2C 30
Old Park La. PO18: Bosh, Fish 6D 14
Old Pl. PO21: Aldw 2F 39
Old Place La. PO18: Westh 6G 5
Old Point PO22: Midd S 6B 32
Old Printing Ho. Sq. BN18: Arun 4C 12
  (off Tarrant St.)
Old Rectory, The PO22: Felp 1F 41
Old Rectory Ct. PO22: Felp 1F 41
  (off Vicarage La.)
Old Rectory Dr. PO20: E'gate 2D 20
Old Rectory Gdns. PO22: Felp 1F 41
Old School M. PO22: Felp 6F 31
Old School Pl. PO20: Westg 3C 20
Old Scotland La. BN18: Bins 5D 10
Old Stables, The PO21: Pag 1E 41
Old Warehouse Mews, The BN17: L'ton 3G 35
  (off Western Rd.)
Oldwick Mdws. PO18: Mid L 2C 4
Old Worthing Rd. BN16: E Pres 6G 27
Olivers Mdw. PO20: Westg 2C 20
Oliver Whitby Rd. PO19: Chich 2A 16
Olivia Cl. PO21: Bog R 2A 40
Olivier Ct. PO21: Bers 5H 29
Olliver Acre BN17: Wick 6F 25
Orchard, The PO21: Aldw 4D 38
Orchard Av. PO19: Chich 2C 16
  PO20: Sel 5E 45
Orchard Bus. Pk. BN18: Yap 5C 22
Orchard Caravan Pk. PO21: Bers 4F 29
Orchard Close, The PO21: Bog R 2A 40
Orchard Cres. BN18: Font 4F 9
Orchard Gdns. BN16: Rust 1C 36
  PO19: Chich 2C 16
  PO20: Westg 4C 20
Orchard La. BN17: Lym 3E 25
  PO20: Sel 3F 45
Orchard Pk. Caravan Site BN16: Rust 6A 26
Orchard Pl. BN18: Font 4C 12
Orchard Rd. BN16: E Pres 1F 37
Orchard St. PO19: Chich 2C 16
Orchard Way BN18: Font 4F 9
  PO22: Barn 3G 21
  PO22: Bog R 6B 30
Oriel Cl. PO22: Barn 3G 21
Orme Cotts. BN16: Ang 3E 27
Ormesby Cres. PO22: Felp 6F 31
Ormonde Av. PO19: Chich 3E 17

Orpen Pl. PO20: Sel 4F 45
Osborn Cl. BN17: Wick 1D 34
Osborn Cres. PO19: Chich 6D 4
Osborne Ct. PO21: Aldw 2C 38
Osborne Cres. PO19: Chich 3G 17
Osborne Way PO21: Aldw 2D 38
Osprey Cl. BN17: Wick 5E 25
Osprey Gdns. PO22: Bers 4B 30
Ostlers, The BN17: L'ton 2E 35
.................................(off Terminus Rd.)
Otard Cl. PO20: Sel 4E 45
Otter Cl. PO19: Chich 1B 16
Otter Gallery, The 1D 16
Otway Rd. PO19: Chich 5D 4
Outerwyke Av. PO22: Felp 5F 31
Outerwyke Gdns. PO22: Felp 5G 31
Outerwyke Rd. PO22: Felp 5F 31
Outram Rd. PO22: Felp 2E 41
Oval La. PO20: Sel 6E 45
Overdown Rd. PO22: Felp 6G 31
Overstrand Av. BN16: Rust 3A 36
OVING 3D 18
Oving Rd. PO19: Chich 3F 17
   PO20: Oving 2G 17
.................................(Chichester By-Pass)
   PO20: Oving 2B 18
.................................(Tangmere Rd.)
   PO20: Oving, Tang, Ald 3D 18
Oving Ter. PO19: Chich 3F 17
Owers Way PO: W Witt 4D 42
Oxford Cl. PO20: W Witt 4E 43
Oxford Dr. PO21: Bog R 1F 39
Oxford St. PO21: Bog R 3A 40
Oxmarket Centre of Arts 3D 16
.................................(off East St.)

P

Pacific Ho. BN16: Rust 3A 36
.................................(off Harsfold Cl.)
Pacific Way PO20: Sel 5E 45
Paddock, The BN17: Lym 3D 24
   PO20: E Witt 5G 43
   PO22: Bog R 6B 30
Paddock Grn. BN16: Rust 1D 36
Paddock La. PO20: Sel 4D 44
Paddocks PO22: Barn 3G 21
PAGHAM 6B 38
Pagham Ct. PO21: Bog R 2H 39
Pagham La. PO20: Lag 3B 28
Pagham Rd. PO20: Lag 5A 38
   PO21: Lag, Pag 5A 38
Pallant House Gallery 3D 16
Palm Ct. BN16: E Pres 3F 37
Palmer Rd. BN16: Ang 3E 27
Palmers Fld. Av. PO19: Chich 1E 17
   PO20: E Witt 4E 43
.................................(off Cakeham Rd.)
Parade, The BN16: E Pres 3F 37
   PO21: Pag 6B 38
Parade Mans. BN16: E Pres 3F 37
.................................(off Willowhayne Cres.)
Parchment St. PO19: Chich 2C 16
Parham Cl. BN16: Rust 3A 36
   BN17: L'ton 1E 35
   PO19: Chich 4F 17
Park Av. PO20: Sel 4F 45
PARK BOTTOM 4A 12
Park Copse PO20: Sel 2H 45
Park Cres. PO20: Sel 3G 45
Park Dr. BN16: Rust 1C 36
   BN18: Yap 1D 32
   PO22: Felp 6A 32
Parker's Cotts. PO18: E Lav 1D 4
Parkfield Av. PO21: Aldw 2E 39
Parklands Av. PO21: Bog R 1A 40
Parklands Rd. PO19: Chich 3B 16
Park La. BN18: Slind 4G 9
   PO18: Hal 2E 7
   PO18: Mid L 3A 4
   PO20: Ald 3A 20
   PO20: Sel 2F 45
Park Pl. BN18: Arun 4B 12
Park Rd. BN18: Yap 1D 32
   PO18: Good 1B 6
   PO20: Sel 3G 45
   PO21: Bog R 3A 40
   PO22: Barn 3A 22
Parkside PO21: Bog R 1C 40
.................................(off Up. Bognor Rd.)
Parkside Av. BN17: L'ton 2G 35
Parkside Ct. BN17: L'ton 2G 35
Park Ter. PO21: Bog R 3A 40
Park Vw. Cl. BN16: Rust 1B 36
Parkway PO21: Bog R 2H 39
Parkway, The BN17: Rust 2C 36
Parry Dr. BN16: Rust 2A 36
Parsons Cl. BN16: Ang 5F 27
Parson's Hill BN18: Arun 4C 12
Parsons Wlk. BN18: Walb 1B 22
Paterson Wilson Rd. BN17: L'ton ...2F 35
Payne Cl. PO21: Pag 5B 38

Peacheries, The PO19: Chich 4F 17
Peachey Rd. PO20: Sel 5D 44
Peacock Cl. PO19: Chich 6E 5
Peak La. BN16: King G 3H 37
Pearson Rd. BN18: Arun 5A 12
Pebble Wlk. BN17: L'ton 6H 25
Peckhams Copse La. PO20: N Mun ...6G 17
Peckham's Copse Trout Fishery 6F 17
Peel Cl. BN17: Wick 1D 34
Peerley Cl. PO20: E Witt 5F 43
Peerley Rd. PO20: E Witt 5F 43
Pembroke Way PO21: Aldw 1F 39
Penfold La. BN16: Rust 6A 26
Penn Cl. PO22: Midd S 6B 32
Pennicott Rd. PO21: Bers 4G 29
Pennycord Cl. PO20: Sel 6E 45
Pennyfields PO22: Felp 6H 31
Penwarden Way PO18: Bosh 2B 14
Pepper Ct. BN17: L'ton 2D 34
.................................(off Terminus Rd.)
Peregrine Rd. BN17: L'ton 1G 35
Peterhouse Cl. PO21: Aldw 1G 39
Peter's Pl. PO20: Sel 3A 44
Peter Weston Pl. PO19: Chich 3E 17
Petts Cl. PO20: Sel 2E 45
Petworth Ct. PO22: Felp 1F 41
.................................(off Felpham Rd.)
Pevensey Rd. PO22: Bog R 1G 39
Pharos Quay BN17: L'ton 2D 34
.................................(off River Rd.)
Phoenix Cl. BN17: Wick 6C 24
   PO19: Chich 4D 16
Picturedrome Cinema
   Bognor Regis 2B 40
Pier Rd. BN17: L'ton 3E 35
Pigeonhouse La. BN16: Rust 3D 36
Piggery Hall La. PO20: W Witt 2E 43
Pilgrims Way PO21: Pag 4C 38
Pine Cl. PO20: Westg 3C 20
Pine Gro. PO19: W Bro 6A 4
Pinehurst Pk. PO21: Aldw 1E 39
Pines, The BN16: Ang 5E 27
   BN18: Yap 6C 22
Pine Trees Cl. BN16: Ang 2E 27
Pine Wlk. PO21: Aldw 1E 39
Pinewood Cl. BN16: E Pres 1F 37
Pinewood Gdns. PO21: Bog R 2H 39
Pitcroft, The PO19: Chich 1F 17
Place St Maur des Fosses PO21: Bog R ...3C 40
.................................(off Belmont St.)
Plainwood Cl. PO19: Chich 5C 4
Plantation, The BN16: E Pres 2F 37
Plover Cl. PO20: E Witt 5F 43
   PO22: Bers 4A 30
POLING 3A 26
POLING CORNER 1A 26
Poling St. BN18: Poling 3H 25
Pond Rd. PO20: Brac 6G 43
Pook La. PO18: E Lav, Mid L 2C 4
Poplars, The BN17: L'ton 6G 25
   BN18: Yap 6D 22
Poplars Caravan Park, The PO22: Bers ...5C 30
Poppy Cl. BN17: L'ton 6H 25
PORTFIELD 2F 17
Portfield Cl. PO19: Chich 2F 17
Portfield Retail Pk. PO19: Chich ...2G 17
Portfield Trad. Est. PO19: Chich ...4G 17
Portfield Way PO19: Chich 1G 17
Portland Cl. BN17: L'ton 1H 35
Potnore PO18: Mid L 1E 5
Potters Grn. PO18: Westh 6H 5
Potters Mead BN17: Wick 6D 24
Poulner Cl. PO22: Felp 6F 31
Pound, The PO21: Aldw 3F 39
Pound Farm Rd. PO19: Chich 3F 17
Pound Rd. BN18: Walb 6A 10
   PO20: W Witt 2A 42
Pound Way BN16: Ang 4F 27
Poyntz Cl. PO19: Chich 6C 16
Prawn Cl. PO20: Sel 3C 44
Precinct, The PO21: Aldw 1G 39
Preston Av. BN16: Rust 2C 36
Preston Hall M. BN16: E Pres 1E 37
.................................(off The Street)
Preston Paddock BN16: Rust 2D 36
Priestley Way PO22: Felp, Midd S ...6A 32
Prime Cl. BN18: Walb 1B 22
Primrose Ct. BN17: L'ton 6H 25
Princes Cft. PO21: Pag 4B 38
Princes Marina Ho. BN16: Rust 4B 36
Princess Av. PO21: Aldw 3H 39
Prior Pl. PO19: Chich 1F 17
Priors Acre PO18: Box 4E 7
Priors Waye PO21: Pag 3B 38
Priory Cl. PO18: Box 4E 7
   PO21: Aldw 5C 38
Priory La. PO19: Chich 2D 16
Priory Park 2D 16
Priory Rd. BN16: Rust 1A 36
   BN18: Arun 6A 12
   PO19: Chich 2D 16

Progress Ho. BN17: L'ton 2E 35
.................................(off Arundel Rd.)
Promenade PO21: Aldw, Bog R 3H 39
   PO22: Felp, Midd S 2F 41
Promenade, The BN17: L'ton 4E 3
Providence, The PO19: Chich 3C 16
Providence Pl. PO19: Chich 3C 16
.................................(off Chapel St.)
Pryors Grn. PO21: Aldw 3D 38
Pryors La. PO21: Aldw 4D 38
Pulborough Way PO22: Felp 5A 32
Purbeck Pl. BN17: L'ton 2D 34
Pyrford Cl. PO21: Pag 3C 38

Q

Quantocks, The BN17: L'ton 1E 35
.................................(off Arundel Rd.)
Quarry La. PO19: Chich 4F 17
Quarry La. Ind. Est. PO19: Chich ...4F 17
Quay Mdw. PO18: Bosh 5A 14
Quayside BN17: L'ton 2C 35
Queen's Av. PO19: Chich 5C 16
Queens Flds. E. PO21: Aldw 1G 39
Queens Flds. W. PO21: Aldw 1F 39
Queens Fld. Wlk. PO21: Aldw 1G 39
Queen's Gdns. PO19: Chich 5C 16
Queens La. BN18: Arun 5C 12
Queensmead PO21: Pag 5A 38
Queen's Sq. PO21: Bog R 2C 40
Queen St. BN17: L'ton 2E 35
   BN18: Arun 4C 12
Queensway PO21: Aldw 4F 39
   PO21: Bog R 2B 40
Quest Cl. PO19: Chich 3E 17

R

Rackham Rd. BN16: Rust 4A 36
Radford Rd. PO21: Bog R 6A 38
Raleigh Rd. PO21: Aldw 2C 38
Ramillies Gdns. PO22: Felp 6H 31
Ranworth Cl. PO22: Felp 6E 31
Ratham La. PO18: Bosh, W Ash 1B 14
Raughmere Ct. PO18: Mid L 2D 4
Raughmere Dr. PO18: Mid L 3C 4
Ravenscroft BN16: Rust 3B 36
.................................(off Sutton Av.)
Ravens Way PO22: Bers 5A 30
Rawson Vs. BN16: Rust 1B 36
Raycroft Cl. PO21: Aldw 3G 39
Rayden Cl. BN17: L'ton 2F 35
Rectory La. BN16: Ang 4E 27
   PO20: Sel 1F 45
Red Barn Cres. PO22: Felp 5F 31
Redhouse Farm Caravan Site PO20: Earn ...3H 43
Red Ridges PO21: Aldw 3H 39
.................................(off King's Pde.)
Redwing Cl. BN17: Wick 5D 24
Redwood Ct. BN17: L'ton 2F 35
Redwood Pl. PO21: Aldw 3F 39
Reef Cl. BN17: L'ton 3G 35
Regents Way PO21: Aldw 1G 39
Regis Av. PO21: Aldw 5C 38
Regis Bus. Cen. PO22: Bers 5C 30
Regis Ct. PO21: Bog R 2C 40
Regis Gate PO21: Bog R 1B 40
Renoir Ct. PO22: Bers 5H 29
Renoir M. PO22: Bers 5H 29
Rew La. PO19: Chich 4C 4
Reynolds La. PO18: Slind 3A 10
Richmond Av. PO19: Chich 6D 4
   PO21: Bog R 2H 39
Richmond Av. W. PO21: Bog R 3H 39
Richmond Cl. BN16: Rust 1D 36
Richmond Ct. BN16: Rust 2A 36
Richmond Ho. PO19: Chich 3D 16
.................................(off Church Sq.)
   PO21: Bog R 2B 40
.................................(off Queensway)
Richmond M. PO22: Shrip 3C 30
Richmond Rd. PO18: Good 4H 5
   PO21: Bog R 2C 40
Richmond Rd. Nth. PO21: Bog R 1C 40
Ridgeway, The PO19: Chich 2B 16
.................................(off Oliver Whitby Rd.)
Ridgway, The PO22: Felp 1G 41
Ridings, The BN16: E Pres 3E 37
   BN18: Font 5F 9
   PO21: Aldw 4D 38
Rife La. PO20: Sel 3B 44
Rife Way PO22: Felp 1E 41
Ripon Gdns. PO21: Aldw 2F 39
River Rd. BN17: L'ton 2D 34
   BN18: Arun 5C 12
Riverside PO19: Chich 2E 17
Riverside Caravan Cen. PO22: Bers ...4C 30
Riverside Ind. Est. BN17: L'ton 2C 34
Robin Cl. BN17: Wick 5D 24
Robins Cl. PO20: Sel 3E 45
Robins Dr. PO21: Aldw 2E 39

bbinson Cl. PO20: Sel 2E 45
bbinson Way PO20: E Witt 5G 43
bchester Cl. PO19: Chich 6C 4
bchester Way PO21: Aldw 2F 39
bckall Cl. BN17: L'ton 6H 25
bckall Way PO18: Bosh 2C 14
bck Gdns. PO21: Bog R 3B 40
(not continuous)
bdney Cl. PO21: Aldw 2D 38
bdney Cres. BN18: Ford 5G 23
bllaston Pk. BN18: Ford 1E 33
bman Amphitheatre 1D 34
bman Av. BN16: Ang 5F 27
bman Flds. PO21: Bog R 1H 39
bman Landing PO20: W Witt 1A 42
bman Way PO19: Fish 3G 15
bmney Broadwalk PO22: Bers 5A 30
bmney Gth. PO20: Sel 4F 45
bokery, The PO20: Sel 3F 45
bokwood Rd. PO20: W Witt 1B 42
bse Av. PO22: Midd S 6C 32
bse Ct. BN17: L'ton 2E 35
(off Gloucester Rd.)
PO21: Aldw 2E 39
OSE GREEN 2E 39
bse Green Art & Craft Cen. 2E 39
(off Rose Grn. Rd.)
bse Grn. Rd. PO21: Aldw 2D 38
bsemary Cl. PO21: Aldw 2D 38
bsemead BN17: L'ton 2F 35
bse Pl. BN17: L'ton 2A 26
bssalyn Cl. PO21: Aldw 2C 38
bss Cl. PO21: Pag 3C 38
bsvara Av. PO20: Westg 2C 20
bundle Av. PO22: Felp 5G 31
bundle Rd. PO22: Felp 6H 31
bundle Sq. PO22: Felp 6G 31
bundle Sq. Rd. PO22: Felp 6G 31
bund Piece PO20: Sel 3C 44
bund Piece La. PO20: Sel 3B 44
bundstone By-Pass BN16: Ang 6E 27
bundstone Cres. BN16: E Pres 1E 37
bundstone Dr. BN16: E Pres 1F 37
bundstone Ho. Caravan Pk.
BN16: E Pres 6F 27
(off Old Worthing Rd.)
bundstone La. BN16: Ang 4F 27
bundstone Way PO20: Sel 3F 45
bundway, The BN16: Rust 3C 36
bwan Way BN16: Ang 5F 27
PO22: Bers 4A 30
byal Cl. PO19: Chich 3F 17
byal Norfolk M. PO21: Bog R 3B 40
(off Norfolk Sq.)
byal Pde. PO21: Bers 5H 29
byce Cl. PO20: W Witt 2B 42
byce Way PO20: W Witt 2B 42
bystons, The BN16: E Pres 3E 37
budford Ind. Est. BN18: Ford 1H 33
budgwick Cl. BN16: Rust 3A 36
budkin Pl. PO18: Fish 1F 15
budwick's Cl. PO22: Felp 1H 41
budwick's Way PO22: Felp 1H 41
buislip Gdns. PO21: Aldw 3D 38
bumbolds Cl. PO19: Chich 4F 17
bummers, The PO19: Chich 5C 4
UNCTON 2A 28
buncton La. PO20: Runc, S Mun 4A 28
bunnymede Ct. PO21: Bog R 6G 29
busbridge Cl. PO21: Aldw 1E 39
buskin Av. PO21: Bers 4H 29
buskin Cl. PO20: Sel 4F 45
bussell Rd. PO20: W Witt 4D 42
bussell's Cl. BN16: E Pres 1G 37
bussell St. PO21: Chich 3F 17
USTINGTON 2B 36
bustington By-Pass BN16: Ang, Rust, L'ton 5A 26
BN17: L'ton 6G 25
bustington Golf Course 5C 26
bustington Mus. 2B 36
bustington Retail Pk. BN16: Rust 6C 26
bustington Trad. Est. BN16: Rust 6B 26
buston Av. BN16: Rust 2C 36
buston Pk. BN16: Rust 2D 36
butland Way PO19: Westh 1G 17
byebank Caravan Site BN18: Bils 4C 32
byefield Rd. PO21: Bers 4G 29

S

back La. PO22: Shrip 1C 30
baddle La. PO20: Sel 4D 44
badlers, The PO18: Westh 6G 5
badler St. PO21: Bog R 3B 40
badlers Wlk. PO19: Chich 3E 17
bt Agnes Pl. PO19: Chich 3E 17
bt Andrew's Cl. PO20: Oving 3D 18

St Andrews Ct. PO19: Chich 3D 16
(off East St.)
St Andrews La. PO20: Tang 6D 6
St Anne's Ct. PO20: E Witt 4E 43
St Anthony's Wlk. PO21: Aldw 2E 39
St Anthonys Way BN16: Rust 1C 36
St Augustine Rd. BN17: L'ton 3F 35
St Bartholomews Cl. PO19: Chich 3B 16
St Blaises Rd. PO18: Box 4D 6
St Catherines Ct. BN17: L'ton 3E 35
St Catherine's Rd. BN17: L'ton 3E 35
St Christopher's Cl. PO19: Chich 3H 15
St Claire Ter. PO21: Bog R 2B 40
St Clares Gdns. PO21: Bers 5H 29
St Clare's M. PO22: Felp 1E 41
St Cyriacs PO19: Chich 2D 16
St Flora's Cl. BN17: L'ton 2G 35
St Flora's Rd. BN17: L'ton 2G 35
St George's Cl. PO20: Sel 3F 45
St George's Dr. PO19: Chich 6C 16
St George's Wlk. PO20: E'gate 2E 21
St Hildas Cl. PO20: Sel 5D 44
St Itha Cl. PO20: Sel 5E 45
St Itha Rd. PO20: Sel 5E 45
St James Ind. Est. PO19: Chich 2F 17
St James Rd. PO19: Chich 2F 17
St James Sq. PO19: Chich 2F 17
St James Works PO19: Chich 2F 17
St Johns Cl. PO20: Ald 4C 20
PO21: Aldw 1G 39
St Johns St. PO19: Chich 3D 16
St Margarets Ct. BN16: Rust 3E 27
St Martin's La. BN17: L'ton 2E 35
(off St Martin's Rd.)
St Martin's Rd. BN17: L'ton 2E 35
St Martins Sq. PO19: Chich 3D 16
St Martins St. PO19: Chich 3D 16
St Marys Cl. BN17: L'ton 2F 35
PO18: Mid L 1F 5
PO22: Bog R 6C 30
St Marys Courtyard PO19: Chich 2D 16
(off St Martins Sq.)
St Mary's Dr. BN16: E Pres 2E 37
St Mary's Gdn. PO19: Chich 3D 16
St Mary's Gdns. BN17: L'ton 2F 35
St Mary's Ga. M. BN18: Arun 4B 12
(off London Rd.)
St Mary's Mdw. BN18: Yap 5C 22
St Mary's Rd. PO18: Box 3D 6
St Marys Way BN17: L'ton 2F 35
St Nicholas Cl. PO22: Midd S 6B 32
St Nicholas La. PO22: Midd S 6C 32
St Nicholas Rd. PO18: Mid L 1B 4
St Pancras PO19: Chich 3E 17
St Pauls Gdns. PO19: Chich 3E 17
St Paul's Rd. PO19: Chich 1B 16
St Peters PO19: Chich 2D 16
St Peters Cl. PO21: Aldw 1F 39
St Peter's Cres. PO20: Sel 3E 45
ST RICHARD'S HOSPITAL 1E 17
St Richards Rd. PO20: Westg 2D 20
St Richard's Wlk. PO19: Chich 3C 16
St Richard's Way PO21: Aldw 2E 39
St Roche's Cl. PO18: Mid L 1F 5
St Thomas Cl. PO21: Pag 5B 38
St Thomas Dr. PO21: Pag 5A 38
St Wilfred's Cl. PO20: Sel 3G 45
St Wilfreds Vw. PO20: Sel 2A 16
St Wilfrid Rd. PO19: Chich 2A 16
ST WILFRID'S HOSPICE 5C 16
St Winefride's Rd. BN17: L'ton 3F 35
St Winifred's Cl. PO21: Bog R 3A 40
Salisbury Way PO19: Chich 6C 4
Saltham La. PO20: Runc 2A 28
Salthill La. PO19: Chich 1H 15
Salthill Pk. PO19: E Ash 1G 15
Salthill Rd. PO19: E Ash, Fish 3G 15
Saltings, The BN17: L'ton 1H 35
Sampsons Dr. PO20: Oving 2D 18
Sanctuary Gdns. PO22: Felp 5F 31
Sandfield Av. PO21: Wick 5E 25
Sandpiper Ct. PO20: E Witt 5F 43
Sandringham Cl. PO20: Brac 6G 43
Sandringham Rd. PO20: Chich 3F 17
Sandringham Way
PO21: Bog R 1A 40
Sandymount Av. PO22: Bog R 6A 30
Sandymount Cl. PO22: Bog R 5B 30
Sandy Point Cl. PO20: Sel 3B 44
Sandy Point La. PO20: Sel 3B 44
Sandy Rd. PO21: Pag 6B 38
Sarisbury Cl. PO22: Felp 6F 31
Satinwood Cl. PO22: Midd S 5B 32
Saxby Cl. PO22: Barn 4G 21
Saxon Cl. BN16: E Pres 6G 27
Saxon Mdw. PO20: Tang 6D 6
Scholars Row PO22: Barn 4H 21
School Cl. PO20: Westg 2D 20
School Hill BN18: Slind 2H 9
School La. BN18: Arun 5C 12
PO18: Bosh 3B 14

School La. PO20: E'gate 2E 21
PO20: Sel 3D 44
Schooner Ct. BN17: L'ton 1H 35
Scott Cl. PO21: Bog R 3B 40
Scotts Farm Caravan & Camping Site
PO20: W Witt 3D 42
Scott St. PO21: Bog R 3B 40
Sea Av. BN16: Rust 3C 36
Seabrook Cl. PO21: Aldw 2E 39
Sea Cl. PO22: Midd S 6B 32
Seacourt Cl. PO21: Aldw 4E 39
Sea Dr. PO22: Felp 1H 41
Seafield Cl. BN16: Rust 3B 36
PO20: E Witt 5F 43
Seafield Rd. BN16: E Pres 3E 37
BN16: Rust 3B 36
Seafields PO20: Brac 6G 43
Seafield Way PO20: E Witt 5F 43
Seagate Cl. PO20: E Witt 5D 42
Seagate Wlk. BN17: L'ton 3H 35
Sea Gro. PO20: Sel 5C 44
Seagull Cl. PO20: Sel 2B 44
Sea La. BN16: E Pres 3E 37
BN16: King G 3H 37
BN16: Rust 3A 36
PO21: Pag 5A 38
PO22: Midd S 6B 32
Seal Cl. BN16: E Pres 2E 37
Seal Rd. PO20: Sel 5D 44
Seal Sq. PO20: Sel 6D 44
Sea Rd. BN16: E Pres 2F 37
BN16: L'ton, Rust 4G 35
BN17: L'ton 4G 35
PO22: Felp 2E 41
Seaton Cl. BN17: Wick 5E 25
Seaton La. BN17: Wick 5E 25
Seaton Pk. BN17: Wick 5E 25
Seaton Rd. BN17: Wick 5E 25
Seaview Av. BN16: E Pres 3F 37
BN16: King G 3H 37
Seaview Ct. PO20: Sel 5D 44
Seaview Gdns. BN16: Rust 3B 36
Seaview Rd. BN16: E Pres 3F 37
Seaward Dr. PO20: W Witt 2B 42
Seawaves Cl. BN16: E Pres 2F 37
Sea Way PO21: Pag 5A 38
PO22: Midd S 6E 33
(Alleyne Way)
PO22: Midd S 6B 32
(Sea La.)
Seawood Ho. PO20: E Witt 4E 43
(off Stocks La.)
Second Av. PO20: Brac 6G 43
PO22: Felp 1G 41
Seddon Cl. PO19: Chich 1F 17
Sefter Rd. PO21: Pag 1C 38
Sefton Av. PO21: Aldw 2E 39
Selborne Pl. BN17: L'ton 3F 35
(off Selborne Rd.)
Selborne Rd. BN17: L'ton 3F 35
Selborne Way BN16: E Pres 2E 37
Selden La. BN13: Pat 1G 27
Selham Cl. PO19: Chich 4D 4
Selhurst Cl. BN16: E Pres 2D 36
SELSEY 4D 44
Selsey Av. PO21: Aldw 3H 39
Selsey Bill 6E 45
Selsey Bus. Cen. PO20: Sel 4D 44
(off The Bridle Way)
Selsey Country Club PO20: Sel 1D 44
Selsey Golf Course 1D 44
Selsey Pl. PO19: Chich 6C 16
PO20: Donn, Sidle 6B 16
Selway La. BN17: L'ton 1G 35
Selwyn Av. BN17: Wick 6E 25
Selwyn Cl. PO21: Aldw 1G 39
Senator Gdns. PO19: Fish 2G 15
Servite Ct. PO21: Bog R 1A 40
Sextant Cl. BN17: L'ton 1H 35
Seymour Pl. PO21: Bog R 2B 40
(off Queensway)
Shaftesbury Ct. BN16: Rust 3B 36
(off Shaftesbury Rd.)
Shaftesbury Pl. BN16: Rust 3B 36
Shaftesbury Rd. BN16: Rust 3B 36
Shalbourne Cres. PO20: Brac 6H 43
Shamrock Cl. PO18: Bosh 4B 14
PO19: Chich 1E 17
Shannon Cl. BN17: L'ton 3H 35
Shardeloes Rd. BN16: Ang 3E 27
Shaw Cl. PO22: Midd S 6D 32
Shaw Gdns. PO21: Bers 4H 29
Shearwater Dr. PO22: Bers 5B 30
Sheep Fold Av. BN16: Rust 1D 36
Sheepwash La. PO18: Mid L 2C 4
Shellbridge Rd. BN18: Slind 3B 10
Shelley Lodge BN17: L'ton 3G 35
Shelley Rd. PO21: Bog R 2A 40
Sherborne Rd. PO19: Chich 3B 16
Sherbourne La. PO20: Sel 3B 44
Sherlock Av. PO19: Chich 2B 16
Sherrington M. PO20: Sel 3F 45
Sherwood Cl. PO22: Bers 5A 30

Sherwood Rd. PO22: Bers 5A 30
Shingle Wlk. PO20: E Witt 5E 43
Ship & Anchor Marina Camping Site
   BN18: Ford 5H 23
Shipfield PO21: Aldw 3G 39
Shippam St. PO19: Chich 3D 16
   (off East Walls)
Shirley Cl. BN16: Rust 3C 36
   PO21: Pag 5B 38
Shirley Dr. PO22: Felp 5F 31
Shirleys Gdn. PO22: Felp 6G 31
Shopfield Cl. BN16: Rust 1B 36
Shop La. PO18: E Lav 2D 4
Shopwhyke Ind. Cen. PO19: Oving 2G 17
Shopwhyke Rd. PO20: Oving 2H 17
SHOPWHYKE .2A 18
Shorecroft PO21: Aldw 4G 39
Shore Rd. PO18: Bosh 5A 14
   (not continuous)
   PO20: E Witt 5D 42
Shoreside Wlk. PO20: E Witt 5E 43
Short Furlong BN17: L'ton 2G 35
SHRIPNEY 2C 30
Shripney Garden Caravan Site PO22: Shrip . . .2B 30
Shripney La. PO22: Bers, Shrip 3B 30
   (not continuous)
Shripney Rd. PO22: Bers, Bog R, Shrip . . .6C 30
   (not continuous)
Shripney Trade Pk. PO22: Bers 5D 30
Shrubbs Dr. PO22: Midd S 6B 32
Sidengreen La. PO18: Good, Westh 4H 5
Sidlaw Ter. PO21: Bog R 2C 40
   (off Clarence Rd.)
Sidlesham Salt Marshes 4F 15
Siggs Ct. PO19: Chich 4F 17
Silver Birch Dr. PO22: Midd S 5B 32
Silverdale Cl. PO21: Pag 5B 38
Silver Lakes PO20: Oving 5B 18
Silverlock Cl. PO19: Chich 1F 17
Silverston Av. PO21: Aldw 3H 39
Silver Way PO20: Brac 6H 43
Silverwood Ct. BN16: Rust 2B 36
Singleton Cl. PO21: Aldw 4C 38
Slattsfield Cl. PO20: Sel 4F 45
SLINDON 2H 9
Slindon Bottom Rd. BN18: Slind 4E 9
SLINDON COMMON 4A 10
Slindon Park 2G 9
Slipe, The BN18: Arun 5C 12
   (off Wheelwrights Cl.)
Sloe Cl. PO19: Chich 2F 17
   (off Story Rd.)
Sloe Gdns. PO22: Felp 5H 31
Smallcroft Cl. BN17: L'ton 2D 34
Snakes La. PO18: Mid L 3B 4
Snowdrop Cl. BN17: L'ton 6A 26
SNOW HILL 1A 42
Solent Cl. BN17: L'ton 6H 25
Solent Rd. PO20: E Witt 5E 43
Solent Way PO20: Sel 6D 44
Solway Cl. BN17: L'ton 2H 35
SOMERLEY 1H 43
Somerset Gdns. PO21: Bog R 6B 30
Somerset Rd. BN16: E Pres 1G 37
Somerstown PO19: Chich 1C 16
Somerton Grn. PO22: Felp 6E 31
South Av. PO21: Aldw 2G 39
South Bank PO19: Chich 5C 16
SOUTH BERSTED 5C 30
Sth. Bersted Ind. Est. PO22: Bers 5C 30
Southcote Av. PO20: W Witt 4D 42
Southcourt Cl. BN16: Rust 1D 36
Southdean Cl. PO22: Midd S 6C 32
Southdean Dr. PO22: Midd S 6C 32
Southdown Cl. PO19: Chich 1F 17
Southdown Ct. PO20: E Witt 4F 43
   (off Stocks La.)
Southdown Rd. PO21: Bog R 2B 40
Sth. Downs Holiday Village PO20: Brac . . .4G 43
South Downs National Pk. 2D 10
South Downs Planetarium 5D 16
South Dr. BN16: Ang 6C 26
   PO22: Felp 6H 31
Southern Cross Ind. Est. PO22: Bers 4D 30
Southern Ga. PO19: Chich 4C 16
Southern Rd. PO20: Sel 5E 45
Southfield Ind. Pk. PO18: Bosh 3A 14
Southfields Cl. PO19: Chich 6C 16
Southfields Rd. BN17: L'ton 2G 35
Southgate PO19: Chich 4C 16
Southlands Ct. BN17: L'ton 3F 35
Southover Rd. PO21: Bog R 2B 40
South Pallant PO19: Chich 3D 16
South Pas. BN17: L'ton 3G 35
South Rd. PO22: Felp 6E 31
South Strand BN16: E Pres 3F 37
South St. PO19: Chich 3D 16
South Ter. BN17: L'ton 3E 35
South Vw. BN16: E Pres 3G 37
Southview Rd. PO22: Felp 1G 41
South Wlk. BN16: E Pres 4D 36
   PO22: Midd S 6A 32
Southwark Wlk. PO21: Aldw 1F 39

South Way PO21: Bers 6H 29
Southway BN17: L'ton 3G 35
Sovereign Ct. PO21: Bog R 2D 40
Sparks Ct. BN17: L'ton 2E 35
Sparshott Rd. PO20: Sel 6E 45
Spencer St. PO21: Bog R 2C 40
   (off Windward Rd.)
Spinnaker Cl. BN17: L'ton 2H 35
Spinney, The BN16: E Pres 3F 37
   PO21: Aldw 2F 39
Spinney Cl. PO20: Sel 3D 44
Spinney Wlk. PO22: Barn 3G 21
Spitalfield La. PO19: Chich 2D 16
Spitfire Ct. PO20: Tang 5E 7
Springbank PO19: Chich 6C 4
Springfield PO21: Pag 3B 38
Springfield Cl. BN16: E Pres 2D 36
   PO18: Mid L 1F 5
Sproule Cl. BN18: Ford 1E 33
Spur Rd. PO19: Chich 4G 17
Square, The BN16: Ang 4E 27
   PO22: Barn 3G 21
Stable Fld. PO22: Midd S 6E 33
Staffords Cl. BN16: Rust 1A 36
Stalham Way PO22: Felp 5F 31
Stammer Ct. BN17: Wick 5G 25
   (off Stammer Rd.)
Stammer Rd. BN17: Wick 5F 25
Stanbrok Cl. PO21: Aldw 2F 39
Stanbury Ct. PO18: Bosh 2B 14
Stane St. PO18: Westh 6G 5
Stanford Cl. PO22: Bog R 6D 30
Stanhope Rd. PO18: Bosh 1F 15
Stanhorn Gro. PO22: Felp 4F 31
Stanley Cl. PO21: Bog R 1C 40
Stanley Ct. PO22: Midd S 5A 32
Stanley Rd. BN17: Wick 6E 25
Stanmore Gdns. PO21: Aldw 3F 39
Stanover La. PO22: Flan 4E 31
   (not continuous)
Stansfield Ct. BN16: Rust 1C 36
   (off Mill La.)
Stanton Dr. PO19: Chich 4C 4
Staple La. PO18: E Lav 1F 5
Stapleton Ct. PO21: Aldw 3E 39
Starboard Wlk. BN17: L'ton 3G 35
Station App. PO19: Chich 4C 16
   PO21: Bog R 2B 40
   (off Longford Rd.)
Station Pde. BN16: E Pres 1D 36
Station Rd. BN16: Ang, E Pres, Rust 1C 36
   BN18: Cross 6D 12
   BN18: Ford 5H 23
   PO18: Bosh 2B 14
   PO21: Bog R 2B 40
Stavely Gdns. PO19: Chich 4C 4
Stean Furlong BN17: Wick 6D 24
Steele Cres. BN17: Wick 5F 25
Stempswood Way PO22: Barn 3G 21
Stephens Cl. PO19: Chich 2F 17
Sterling Pde. BN16: Rust 2B 36
Sternway BN17: L'ton 2H 35
Stewards Ri. BN18: Arun 6A 12
Steyne, The PO21: Bog R 3B 40
Steyne St. PO21: Bog R 2B 40
Steyning Way PO22: Bers 4D 30
Stirling Rd. PO19: Chich 3D 16
Stirling Way PO21: Aldw 3F 39
STOCKBRIDGE .5C 16
Stockbridge Gdns. PO19: Chich 6B 16
Stockbridge Pl. PO19: Chich 5C 16
   (off Stockbridge Rd.)
Stockbridge Rd. PO19: Chich 5C 16
Stockbridge Rdbt. PO19: Chich 5C 16
Stocker Rd. PO21: Bog R 3A 40
Stocks La. PO18: E Lav, Westh 3E 5
   PO20: E Witt 4E 43
Stocke Clump PO20: Sel 2E 45
Stoneage Cl. PO22: Bers 4B 30
Stonefields BN16: Rust 2C 36
Stonehill Cres. PO21: Bog R 2C 38
Stoney Stile Cl. PO21: Aldw 3D 38
Stoney Stile La. PO21: Aldw 4D 38
Storrington Cl. PO19: Fish 1G 15
Story Rd. PO19: Chich 2F 17
Strand Ct. BN16: Rust 4F 36
   (off Harsfold Rd.)
Strand Way PO22: Felp 1G 41
Strange Gdn. PO21: Aldw 4F 39
Stratford Pl. PO21: Bog R 2B 40
   (off Victoria Dr.)
Stratton Ct. PO22: Bog R 6B 30
Stream Cl. PO18: Bosh 4A 14
Streatheigh Ct. PO21: Aldw 3H 39
   (off King's Pde.)
Street, The BN16: E Pres 1E 37
   BN16: Rust 2A 36
   BN18: Walb 6A 10
   PO18: Box 3E 7
Streete Ct. PO21: Bog R 3A 40
STRETTINGTON .4B 6
Strettington La. PO18: Box 3B 6

Stride Cl. PO19: Chich 3F 1
Stroud Grn. Dr. PO21: Bers 6G 2
Strouds La. PO21: Bers 6G 2
Stubcroft La. PO20: Sel 5G 4
Stumps End PO18: Bosh 5B 1
Stumps La. PO18: Bosh 5B 1
Sturges Rd. PO21: Bog R 2B 4
Sudbury Ct. PO21: Aldw 4D 3
Sudley Gdns. PO21: Bog R 2C 4
Sudley Rd. PO21: Bog R 2C 4
Summerfield Rd. PO20: W Witt 1A 4
Summerhill Cl. PO22: Felp 5H 3
Summerhill Dr. PO22: Felp 5H 3
Summer La. PO21: Pag 4A 3
Summerlea Gdns. BN17: L'ton 2F 3
Summerley Cl. BN16: Rust 6A 2
Summerley Cnr. PO22: Felp 1G 4
   (off Summerley La.)
Summerley La. PO22: Felp 6G 31
Summers Cl. BN16: Rust 3B 36
SUMMERSDALE .5C
Summersdale Ct. PO19: Chich 4C 4
Summersdale Rd. PO19: Chich 6D 4
Sundale La. PO22: Midd S 6B 32
Sunderland Cl. PO20: Tang 5E 7
Sunflower Cl. BN17: L'ton 5A 26
Sunningdale Gdns. PO20: W Witt 4C 42
   PO22: Bers 4A 30
Sunnybox La. BN18: Slind 3A 10
Sunnymead Cl. PO20: Sel 5F 45
   PO22: Midd S 5D 32
Sunnymead Dr. PO20: Sel 5E 45
Sunnyside Cl. BN16: Rust 5F 27
Sunnyway PO18: Bosh 4A 14
Sun Pk. Cl. PO21: Bers 5H 29
Surrey Cl. BN18: Arun 5B 12
   (off Surrey St.)
Surrey St. BN17: L'ton 3E 35
   BN18: Arun 5B 12
Surrey Wharf BN18: Arun 5C 12
Sussex Bus. Village, The PO22: Barn 3B 22
Sussex Ct. PO22: Midd S 6E 33
Sussex Dr. PO21: Pag 4B 38
Sussex Gdns. BN16: Rust 1B 36
Sussex Gro. PO20: Brac 6H 43
Sussex Pl. PO21: Bog R 2C 40
   (off High St.)
Sussex St. BN17: Wick 1E 35
   PO21: Bog R 2C 40
Sussex Village PO22: Midd S 6E 33
   (off Manor Way)
Sutherland Cl. BN16: Rust 2A 36
   PO21: Bog R 2B 40
Sutherland Ct. PO21: Bog R 2B 40
   (off Sutherland Cl.)
Sutton Av. BN16: Rust 3B 36
Sutton Cl. PO22: Felp 5E 31
Swallows, The BN17: L'ton 3E 35
Swallow Way PO20: Sel 2E 45
Swanbourne Lake 2C 12
Swanbourne Rd. BN17: Wick 6E 25
Swan Dene PO21: Pag 6A 38
Swanfield Dr. PO19: Chich 2E 17
Swansea Gdns. PO21: Bog R 3A 40
Swanwick Wlk. BN17: Wick 1D 34
   (off Manning Rd.)
Swift Way BN17: Wick 5D 24
Swillage La. BN13: Pat 1F 27
Sycamore Cl. BN16: Ang 5E 27
Sycamore Rd. PO22: Bers 4B 30
Sycamores, The PO19: Chich 2D 16
   (off Spitalfield La.)
Syke Cluan Cl. PO22: Barn 3G 21
Sylvan Way PO21: Bog R 2A 40
Sylvia Cl. PO21: Pag 4B 38

T

Tabard Ga. PO21: Pag 4C 38
Tack Lee Rd. BN18: Yap 6C 22
Talbot Rd. BN17: L'ton 2D 34
Taldua Pl. PO21: Bog R 3A 40
Tamarisk Cl. PO22: Bers 5B 30
Tamarisk Wlk. PO20: E Witt 5D 42
Tamarisk Way BN16: E Pres 3D 36
Tamar Way PO20: Tang 6E 7
TANGMERE 5E 7
Tangmere Ct. BN16: Rust 3B 36
   (off Seafield Rd.)
Tangmere Gdns. PO21: Aldw 3E 39
Tangmere Military Aviation Mus. 6E 7
Tangmere Rd. PO20: Tang, Oving 5D 6
Tannery Cl. PO19: Chich 3B 16
Tarrant Sq. BN18: Arun 4C 12
   (off Tarrant St.)
Tarrant St. BN18: Arun 5C 12
Tarrant Wharf BN18: Arun 5C 12
Tarz La. PO20: Donn 6B 16
Tasman Cl. BN16: Rust 3C 36
Taverner Pl. PO19: Chich 4E 17
Taylor Cl. BN16: Rust 6A 26
Taylors Cl. BN18: Yap 2C 32

ylor's La. PO18: Bosh 5B 14
  PO20: Oving 3B 18
eal La. PO20: Sel 3C 44
easel Gro. PO22: Felp 5H 31
emplars Cl. PO22: Midd S 5A 32
EMPLE BAR .4B 6
emple Bar Bus. Pk. PO18: Box 4B 6
emplesheen Rd. PO22: Midd S 6E 33
enacre Cl. PO19: Chich 1F 17
ennyson Av. BN16: Rust 2H 35
ennyson Rd. PO21: Bog R 2H 39
erminus Mill PO19: Chich 4C 16
erminus Pl. BN17: L'ton 2E 35
erminus Rd. BN17: L'ton 2D 34
  PO19: Chich 4A 16
erminus Rd. Ind. Est. PO19: Chich 4B 16
errace, The BN18: Cross 6F 13
eulon Ct. BN16: Ang 6E 27
hakeham Cl. BN16: E Pres 6G 27
hames Cl. BN17: L'ton 3H 35
hatchway, The BN16: Ang 4D 26
  BN16: Rust .3C 36
hatchway Cl. BN17: Wick 1E 35
he . . . .
  Names prefixed with 'The' for example
  'The Acorns' are indexed under the main
  name such as 'Acorns, The'
heatre La. PO19: Chich 3D 16
hicket La. PO18: Eart 1H 7
hicketts, The PO21: Aldw 1D 38
hird Av. PO20: Brac 6G 43
  PO22: Felp .1G 41
hirlmere Way PO22: Felp 5G 31
histle Copse PO22: Felp 5H 31
              (off Blackthorn Av.)
hompson Rd. PO22: Midd S 6C 32
horgate Rd. BN17: Wick 6C 24
horncroft Rd. BN17: L'ton 1F 35
horndene Av. PO21: Bog R 1A 40
horney Dr. PO20: Sel 4C 44
hornlea Pk. BN17: Wick 4D 24
hornton Ct. BN16: Rust 1D 36
hrumley Copse PO20: Sel 2E 45
hrusloes PO21: Aldw 3G 39
ide Way PO20: Brac 6H 43
ideway BN17: L'ton 3H 35
ile Barn La. PO20: E Witt 2H 43
ilemakers Cl. PO18: Westh 6H 5
ilford Dr. PO22: Bers 5D 30
imberlaine Ind. Est. PO19: Chich 4F 17
imberleys BN17: L'ton 6G 25
inghall PO21: Aldw 2F 39
inwood La. PO18: Box 2F 7
ithe Barn Chalets PO20: Sel 3B 44
           (off Montalan Av.)
ithe Barn Cl. PO21: Aldw 4D 38
ithe Barn Ct. PO21: Aldw 4D 38
ithe Barn Way PO21: Aldw 4C 38
ithe Grn. BN16: Rust 2A 36
ODDINGTON .5F 25
oddington La. BN17: Wick 5F 25
oddington Pk. BN17: Wick 5F 25
oe End PO20: Sel 2A 44
ollhouse Cl. PO19: Chich 3C 16
op Rd. BN18: Slind 1H 9
ORTINGTON .2H 23
ortington La. BN18: Tort 1H 23
ortington Mnr. BN18: Tort 2H 23
orton Hill Rd. BN18: Arun 5A 12
ourist Info. Cen.
  Arundel 4D 12
  Bognor Regis 3C 40
  Chichester .3C 16
  Littlehampton 3E 35
ower Cl. PO19: Chich 2C 16
ower Ho. Gdns. BN18: Arun 4C 12
ower Pl. PO20: E Witt 4E 43
ower St. PO19: Chich 2C 16
own Cross Av. PO21: Bog R 1B 40
own La. PO18: Box 4C 6
own Quay BN18: Arun 4C 12
              (off River Rd.)
ownsend Cres. BN17: L'ton 1G 35
ozer Way PO19: Chich 3E 17
rafalgar Ct. PO21: Bog R 3A 40
           (off Victoria Rd.)
regarth Rd. PO19: Chich 5D 4
rendle Grn. PO21: Aldw 2G 39
retawn Gdns. PO20: Sel 5F 45
rinity Way BN17: L'ton 3G 35
  PO21: Aldw 1G 39
riton Pl. PO22: Felp 6H 31
rotyn Cft. PO21: Aldw 2G 39
rue Blue Pct. BN17: Wick 6E 25
rundle Cl. PO18: Mid L 1B 4
rundle Vw. Cl. PO22: Barn 3G 21
ruro Cl. PO21: Aldw 6C 4
ruro Cres. PO21: Aldw 2F 39
ryndel Way PO22: Felp 1G 41
udor Cl. PO19: Chich 5C 4
  PO22: Midd S 6A 32
udor Dr. PO20: Westg 1C 20
upper Gdns. PO22: Felp 5F 31

Turnbull Rd. PO19: Chich 2E 17
Turner Way PO20: Sel 4F 45
Turnpike Cl. PO19: Chich 6B 16
Turret Ho. PO22: Felp 1F 41
             (off Limmer La.)
Turret Ho. M. PO22: Felp 1F 41
             (off Limmer La.)
Tuscan Av. PO22: Midd S 6C 32
Two Barns La. PO18: Mid L 1A 4
Tye La. BN18: Walb 6B 10
Tyne Way PO21: Aldw 1E 39
Tythe Barn Rd. PO20: Sel 5E 45

U

Ullswater Dr. BN17: L'ton 6H 25
Ullswater Gro. PO22: Felp 5G 31
University of Chichester
  Bishop Otter Campus 1E 17
  Bognor Regis Campus 1D 40
Uppark Way PO22: Felp 5A 32
Up. Bognor Rd. PO21: Bog R, Felp 1C 40
Upper Dr. BN16: E Pres 3G 37
Upton Rd. PO19: Chich 5C 16
Upways Cl. PO20: Sel 2E 45
Ursula Av. PO20: Sel 5D 44
           (not continuous)
Ursula Av. Nth. PO20: Sel 5D 44
Ursula Sq. PO20: Sel 6D 44

V

Valdoe Trundle PO20: Sel 2E 45
Valentines Gdns. PO21: Aldw 3D 38
Van Dyck Pl. PO22: Bers 5H 29
Van Gogh Pl. PO22: Bers 5A 30
Velyn Av. PO19: Chich 3E 17
Ventura PO22: Bers 5B 30
Verica Ct. PO19: Fish 2G 15
Vermont Dr. BN16: E Pres 2F 37
Vermont Way BN16: E Pres 2F 37
Vernon Cl. BN16: Rust 2B 36
Veronica Cl. BN16: E Pres 3F 37
Via Ravenna PO19: Chich 3B 16
Via Ravenna Rdbt. PO19: Chich 4C 16
Vicarage La. BN16: E Pres 2E 37
  PO22: Felp .1E 41
Vicars Cl. PO19: Chich 3D 16
Victoria Dr. PO21: Bog R 3A 40
Victoria Gdns. BN17: L'ton 3E 35
             (off Clifton Rd.)
  PO20: Westg 2C 20
Victoria M. PO21: Bog R 1B 40
             (off Victoria Dr.)
Victorian Bus. Cen. BN18: Ford 5G 23
Victoria Pl. PO21: Bog R 3A 40
Victoria Rd. PO19: Chich 3F 17
  PO21: Bog R 3A 40
Victoria Rd. Sth. PO21: Bog R 3A 40
Victoria Rd. BN18: Yap 1D 32
Victory Ct. PO21: Bog R 3A 40
             (off Aldwick Rd.)
View, The PO21: Pag 5B 38
             (off Surrey St.)
Viking Ct. BN17: L'ton 3E 35
Viking Way PO18: Bosh 4A 14
Villa Pl. PO22: Midd S 6D 32
Vincent Rd. PO20: Sel 5C 44
Vinery, The BN18: Poling 1B 26
Vinnetrow Bus. Pk. PO19: Runc 6H 17
Vinnetrow Rd. PO20: Runc 5G 17
Virginia Gdns. PO22: Felp 5H 31
Viscount Dr. PO21: Pag 5C 38

W

Wad, The PO20: W Witt 2A 42
Wade End PO20: Sel 3C 44
Wadeway, The PO20: Sel 3C 44
Wadhurst Cl. PO21: Bog R 1A 40
Wakefield Way PO21: Aldw 1F 39
Wakehurst Pl. BN16: Rust 1B 36
WALBERTON .1B 22
Walberton Cl. PO22: Felp 6F 31
WALBERTON GREEN 6H 9
Walders Rd. BN16: Rust 1A 36
Walkway, The BN16: Ang 5F 27
Wallace Rd. BN16: Rust 6B 26
Wall Cott. Dr. PO19: Chich 3C 16
Wallfield PO21: Aldw 4G 39
Wallner Cres. PO22: Felp 6H 31
Walls Wlk. PO19: Chich 3D 16
             (off Friary La.)
Walmsleys Way PO20: Brac 6H 43
Walnut Av. BN16: Rust 2A 36
  PO19: Chich 1B 16
Walnut Tree Caravan Pk. PO20: W Witt 1B 42
Walsham Cl. PO22: Felp 5E 31
Walters Grn. BN17: Wick 4D 24
Walton Av. PO21: Bog R 2D 40

Walton Cl. PO18: Bosh 4B 14
Walton Rd. PO21: Bog R 2C 40
Wandleys Caravan Pk. PO20: E'gate 6E 9
Wandleys Cl. PO20: E'gate 6E 9
Wandleys Dr. PO20: E'gate 6E 9
Wandleys La. BN18: E'gate, Walb 6E 9
  PO20: E'gate, Walb 6E 9
Wansford Way PO22: Felp 1H 41
Warbleheath Cl. PO18: Mid L 1C 4
Warblers Way PO22: Bers 4A 30
Warner Farm Touring Pk. PO20: Sel 2C 44
Warner La. PO20: Sel 3B 44
Warner Rd. PO20: Sel 5C 44
WARNINGCAMP 4F 13
Warningcamp La. BN18: W'camp 4F 13
Warren Cres. BN16: E Pres 1E 37
Warren Farm La. PO19: Chich 5C 4
Warren Way PO22: Barn 3G 21
Warwick Cl. PO21: Pag 3C 38
Warwick Ct. BN18: Arun 5B 12
Warwick Pl. PO22: Felp 6A 32
Washington St. PO19: Chich 2C 16
WATERBEACH .2B 6
Water Fld. Gdns. PO19: Chich 3H 15
Waterford Gdns. BN17: Climp 2G 33
Water La. BN13: Ang 3G 27
  BN16: Ang 4E 27
  BN17: Wick .1E 35
Waterloo Rd. PO22: Felp 1F 41
Waterloo Sq. PO21: Bog R 3B 40
Waterplat, The PO19: Chich 1F 17
Waters Edge PO21: Aldw 4F 39
Watersedge Gdns. PO20: W Witt 5D 42
Waterside, The BN17: L'ton 2D 34
             (off River Rd.)
Waterside Dr. PO19: Chich 6C 16
Watersmead Bus. Pk. BN17: L'ton 5G 25
Watersmead Cl. BN17: L'ton 6H 25
Watersmead Dr. BN17: L'ton 6H 25
Watersmeet PO19: Chich 3H 15
Watery La. PO19: Huns 6D 16
           (not continuous)
Watson Way PO20: Westg 2C 20
Waverley Rd. BN16: Rust 2B 36
  PO21: Bog R 1H 39
Way, The BN16: E Pres 3F 37
Wayside Rd. BN16: Ang 5F 27
Wealden Dr. PO18: Westh 6H 5
Weavers Hill BN16: Ang 4F 27
Weavers Ring BN16: Ang 4F 27
Webb Cl. PO21: Pag 6B 38
Wedgwood Rd. PO22: Felp 1F 41
Wellers Cl. PO22: Felp 5F 31
Wellington Gdns. PO20: Sel 3E 45
Wellington Pl. PO20: Tang 5E 7
Wellington Rd. PO19: Chich 6D 4
  PO21: Bog R 2A 40
Well Rd. PO21: Bog R 6A 38
Wells Cres. PO19: Chich 6B 4
  PO21: Aldw 2E 39
Wellsfield PO20: W Witt 2B 42
Wendy Ridge BN16: Rust 1A 36
Wentworth Cl. PO22: Barn 2G 21
Wentworth Ct. BN16: E Pres 3F 37
            (off The Nookery)
WEPHAM 2H 13
Wessex Av. PO20: E Witt 4F 43
  PO21: Aldw 3H 39
West Av. PO21: Aldw 2G 39
  PO22: Midd S 5C 32
West Bank BN18: Yap 4D 22
West Beach PO20: W Witt 4C 42
West Beach Local Nature Reserve 4D 34
W. Beach Rd. PO20: W Witt 4C 42
W. Bracklesham Dr. PO20: E Witt 5F 43
Westbridge Path PO18: Mid L 3B 4
Westbrook Cl. PO18: Bosh 4A 14
Westbrook Fld. PO18: Bosh 4A 14
W. Brook Way PO22: Felp 5H 31
WEST BROYLE .5A 4
West Cl. PO22: Felp 1G 41
  PO22: Midd S 6A 32
West Dr. BN16: Ang 5C 26
  PO21: Aldw 4C 38
  PO22: Midd S 6D 32
WESTERGATE .2C 20
Westergate M. PO20: Westg 1C 20
Westergate St. PO20: Westg 4C 20
Westerley Gdns. PO20: E Witt 5G 43
             (off Plover Cl.)
Western Rd. BN17: L'ton 3F 35
  PO20: Sel 5E 45
WESTERTON 4A 6
Westfield PO22: Bers 4A 30
Westfield Av. BN16: E Pres 3F 37
Westgate PO19: Chich 3A 16
Westgate Leisure Cen. 3C 16
Westgate Link Rdbt. PO19: Chich 3A 16
Westgate Rdbt. PO19: Chich 3C 16
WESTHAMPNETT 6H 5
Westhampnett Rd. PO19: Chich 2F 17
West Head BN17: L'ton 3G 35

Westingway PO21: Bog R 2H 39
WEST KINGSTON 3H 37
Westlands BN16: Rust 1H 35
WEST LAVANT 2A 4
Westloats Gdns. PO21: Bog R 6A 30
Westloats La. PO21: Bog R 6H 29
West Mead BN16: E Pres 3D 36
Westmead Rd. PO19: Chich 3H 15
Westminster Dr. PO21: Aldw 2E 39
Westmorland Dr. PO22: Felp 5G 31
Westmount Caravan Pk. PO20: Sel 3D 44
West Pallant PO19: Chich 3D 16
WEST PRESTON 1D 36
W. Preston M. BN16: Rust 2D 36
                                    (off Station La.)
West Ridings BN16: E Pres 3D 36
W. Sands Caravan Pk. PO20: Sel 3A 44
                                    (not continuous)
W. Sands La. PO20: Sel 3B 44
W. Stoke Rd. PO18: Mid L 4A 4
    PO19: W Bro 4A 4
West Strand PO20: W Witt 3A 42
West St. PO19: Chich 3C 16
    PO20: Sel 5C 44
    PO21: Bog R 3B 40
West Vw. Dr. BN18: Yap 1C 32
West Vw. Gdns. BN18: Yap 2C 32
W. Walberton La. BN18: Walb 5G 9
West Wlk. BN16: E Pres 3D 36
Westward Cl. PO18: Bosh 4B 14
Westward Ho. PO19: Chich 3H 15
                             (off Fishbourne Rd. (East))
West Way PO19: Fish 3G 15
    PO19: W Bro 6A 4
Westway BN17: Wick 6D 24
    PO22: Bog R 6C 30
WEST WITTERING .1B 42
Whapple, The BN17: L'ton 3H 35
Wharf Rd. BN17: L'ton 2D 34
Wheatcroft BN17: Wick 6D 24
Wheatfield PO20: Sel 3F 45
Wheelwrights Cl. BN18: Arun 5B 12
Whistler Av. PO19: Chich 6D 4
Whitaker Pl. PO20: Oving 2C 18
White Acre BN17: Wick 6D 24
White Beam Way PO20: Tang 6E 7
Whitebeam Way PO22: Midd S 5B 32
Whitecroft BN16: Rust 2B 36
White Horse Caravan Pk. PO20: Sel 3D 44
White Horses Way BN17: L'ton 2H 35
Whitelands PO22: Felp 5F 31
Whitelea Rd. BN17: Wick 1E 35
White Lodge BN17: L'ton 2F 35
Whiteside Cl. PO19: Chich 2E 17
Whiteways PO22: Bers 5H 29
Whiteways Cl. BN17: L'ton 1E 35
    PO22: Bers 5H 29
Whitfield Cl. BN16: Ang 5F 27
    PO22: Bog R 6D 30
WHYKE 3E 17
Whyke Cl. PO19: Chich 5E 17
Whyke Ct. PO19: Chich 5E 17
Whyke La. PO19: Chich 3E 17
Whyke Marsh PO19: Chich 5E 17
Whyke Rd. PO19: Chich 3E 17
Whyke Rdbt. PO19: Chich 5E 17
WICK 6E 25
Wickbourne Ho. BN17: Wick 1D 34
                                    (off Clun Rd.)
Wick Cl. PO22: Felp 6G 31
Wick Ct. BN17: Wick 6C 24
                                    (off Phoenix Cl.)
Wick Farm Rd. BN17: Wick 1D 34
Wick La. PO22: Felp 6G 31
Wick Pde. BN17: Wick 6E 25
Wick St. BN17: Wick 1E 35
Widgeon La. PO20: Sel 3B 44
Wight Ct. BN17: L'ton 3E 35
Wight Way PO20: Sel 6E 45

Wilkinson Cl. BN16: Ang 4F 27
William Booker Yd. BN18: Walb 6B 10
William Cawley M. PO19: Chich 2D 16
William Olders Rd. BN16: Ang 5F 27
William Rd. PO19: Chich 3G 17
Williams Rd. PO18: Bosh 2B 14
William St. PO21: Bog R 2C 40
Willow Av. BN16: Rust 2D 36
Willowbed Av. PO19: Chich 5F 17
Willowbed Dr. PO19: Chich 5E 17
Willow Brook BN17: Wick 6D 24
Willowbrook PO22: Midd S 6D 32
Willow Ct. BN16: Rust 1B 36
    PO19: Chich 3A 16
Willowhale Av. PO21: Aldw 3E 39
Willowhale Grn. PO21: Aldw 3D 38
Willowhayne Av. BN16: E Pres 3G 37
                                    (Coastal Rd.)
    BN16: E Pres 3F 37
                               (Willowhayne Cres.)
Willowhayne Cl. BN16: E Pres 3F 37
Willowhayne Cres. BN16: E Pres 3F 37
Willowhayne M. PO21: Aldw 2D 36
Willowmead Cl. PO20: Runc 2A 28
Willows, The BN16: Rust 1C 36
    BN18: Ford 4H 23
    PO20: Sel 3E 45
                                    (Mnr. Farm Ct.)
    PO20: Sel 2E 45
                                    (The Links)
Willows Caravan Site PO20: W'gate 5D 20
Willow Way PO21: Aldw 4C 38
Willowwood Cl. BN16: Ang 5F 27
Wills Cl. BN18: Ford 1E 33
Wilman Gdns. PO21: Aldw 3E 39
Wilson Cl. PO19: Chich 2A 16
Wilson Ct. BN18: Ford 1E 33
Wilton Cl. BN16: Rust 6A 26
    PO20: Brac 6H 43
Wilton Dr. BN16: Rust 6A 26
Wiltshire Cft. Ct. PO20: Sel 4D 44
Winchester Dr. PO19: Chich 1C 16
Winchester Rd. BN16: Rust 1D 36
Winden Av. PO19: Chich 3E 17
Windlesham Ct. BN17: Wick 5E 25
Windlesham Gdns. BN16: E Pres 1F 37
Windmill, The 4E 35
Windmill Cl. BN16: Ang 5F 27
    PO21: Aldw 4C 38
Windmill Ct. PO20: E Witt 4E 43
    PO20: Tang 6E 7
    PO22: Barn 4G 21
Windmill Dr. BN16: Rust 1C 36
    PO20: Tang 5E 7
Windmill Fld. PO18: Bosh 4A 14
Windmill Rd. BN17: L'ton 4E 35
Windsor Cl. BN16: Rust 6A 26
    PO21: Aldw 1F 39
Windsor Dr. BN16: Rust 6A 26
    PO20: W Witt 4D 42
Windsor Rd. PO19: Chich 3F 17
    PO20: Sel 5E 45
Windward Cl. BN17: L'ton 2H 35
Windward Rd. PO18: Bosh 4A 14
Wingard Way PO19: Chich 4D 16
Winston Cl. PO21: Bers 5G 29
Winston Cres. PO21: Bers 5G 29
Winterbourne Rd.
    PO19: Chich 5D 4
Winter Knoll, The BN17: L'ton 3G 35
Winterton Lodge BN17: L'ton 2F 35
Wish Fld. Dr. PO22: Felp 5G 31
Wiston Av. PO19: Chich 5B 16
Witham Ct. PO21: Bog R 6A 30
Wittering Wlk. PO20: E Witt 4E 43
Woking Ct. BN16: Rust 1D 36
WOLDHURST 3A 28
Wolfe Cl. PO19: Chich 6C 4
Wolsey Cl. PO21: Pag 4C 38

Wolstenbury Rd. BN16: Rust 6B 2
Woodborough Cl. PO20: Brac 6H
Woodbridge Pk. BN16: E Pres 2F
Woodcote La. BN17: Wick 4E 2
Woodend PO21: Bog R 1H
Woodfield Cl. PO20: Tang 6E
    PO21: Pag 6B
WOODGATE 4C
Woodgate Cl. PO20: W'gate 4C 2
Woodgate Pk. PO20: Westg 3C
Woodgate Rd. PO20: W'gate 4C
Wood Hill Ct. PO22: Felp 5G
                                    (off Wish Fld. D
Wood Hill Way PO22: Felp 5G
Woodhorn La. PO20: Oving 2E
Woodland Rd. PO20: Sel 6D
Woodlands Av. BN16: Rust 2B
Woodlands Cl. BN16: Ang 2F
    BN16: Rust 1B
Woodlands Cotts. BN16: Rust 1B
Woodlands La. PO19: Chich 1C
Woodlands Pk. BN18: Yap 6C 2
Woodlands Rd. BN17: L'ton 3F
    PO22: Bers 5A
Woodruff Bus. Cen. PO19: Chich 4B
Woodside PO21: Aldw 3G
Woodstock Gdns. PO21: Aldw 3G
Wood St. PO21: Bog R 3A
Wood Vw. BN18: Arun 5B
Wooldridge Wlk. BN17: Climp 2G
Woolstaplers, The
    PO19: Chich 3C
Worcester Cl. PO21: Aldw 2F
Worcester Rd. PO19: Chich 6C
Wordsworth Gdns. PO22: Felp 5A
Worms La. PO22: Felp, Midd S 4H
Worthing Rd. BN16: E Pres 1E
    BN16: Rust 6H
    BN17: L'ton, Wick 6E
Wren Cres. PO22: Bers 5A
Wrenfield Pl. PO21: Bog R 3B
                                    (off Scott C
Wroxham Way PO22: Felp 5E
Wyatt Ct. PO20: E Witt 4E
Wychcroft BN17: L'ton 2E
                                    (off Linden Ro
Wychwood Cl. PO21: Aldw 4F
Wychwood Wlk. PO21: Aldw 4F
Wyde Feld PO21: Aldw 3G
Wyke La. Nth. PO22: Felp 5H
Wythering Cl. PO21: Pag 6A
Wyvern Cl. PO20: Tang 6F

Y

YAPTON 6C 2
Yapton La. BN18: Walb 5C
Yapton Rd. BN17: Climp 1E 3
    BN18: Bils 4C 3
    BN18: Ford, Climp 1E 3
    BN18: Yap 4H 2
    PO22: Barn 5A
    PO22: Midd S 6B 3
Yarbrook PO18: Mid L 1E
Yeomans Acre PO21: Aldw 2G 3
Yew Tree Cl. PO22: Bers 5A 3
York Chase PO19: Chich 5C
York Gdns. BN17: L'ton 2E 3
York Rd. BN17: L'ton 2E 3
    PO19: Chich 4F 1
    PO20: Sel 6E 4
    PO21: Bog R 2C 4
Young St. PO19: Chich 6D

Z

ZACHARY MERTON HOSPITAL 3C 3
Zola Pk. Retail Pk. PO19: Chich 1F 1

SAFETY CAMERA INFORMATION

PocketGPSWorld.com's CamerAlert is a self-contained speed and red light camera warning system for SatNavs and Android or Apple iOS smartphones/tablets. Visit www.cameralert.co.uk to download.

Safety camera locations are publicised by the Safer Roads Partnership which operates them in order to encourage drivers to comply with speed limits at these sites. It is the driver's absolute responsibility to be aware of and to adhere to speed limits at all times.

By showing this safety camera information it is the intention of Geographers' A-Z Map Company Ltd., to encourage safe driving and greater awareness of speed limits and vehicle speed. Data accurate at time of printing.